TALKS AND HOW TO GIVE THEM

or

Say What You Mean

COMPANION VOLUMES

REPORTS AND HOW TO WRITE THEM

H. A. Shearring and B. C. Christian

SECOND PRINTING

COMMITTEES

How They Work and How to Work Them

Edgar Anstey

SECOND PRINTING

TALKS AND HOW TO GIVE THEM

or

SAY WHAT YOU MEAN

H. A. Shearring, M.A., D.PHIL.
and
B. C. Christian, B.SC., PH.D., F.R.I.C.

LONDON
George Allen and Unwin Ltd
RUSKIN HOUSE   MUSEUM STREET

FIRST PUBLISHED IN 1970
SECOND IMPRESSION 1971

SBN: 04 808009 8 *cased*
04 808010 1 *paper*

PRINTED IN GREAT BRITAIN BY
REDWOOD PRESS LIMITED, TROWBRIDGE & LONDON

CONTENTS

Speech Can Be Golden

Speech is silver, silence is golden.

'The most serious problem in external relationships is probably the need to develop efficient means for communicating ideas and results of research to executive users. The more experienced operations research groups have come to realize that explaining or "selling" conclusions is just as important as arriving at conclusions, if they are to be useful.'

Herrmann and Magee: 'Operations Research for Management', *Harvard Business Review,* July/August 1953

'Behold, we put bits in the horses' mouths, that they may obey us; and we turn about their whole body.

Behold also the ships, which though they be so great, and are driven of fierce winds, yet are they turned about with a very small helm, whithersoever the governor listeth.

Even so the tongue is a little member, and boasteth great things. Behold, how great a matter a little fire kindleth!'

The General Epistle of James, Chapter 3

It is little use to be right if you cannot convince other people that you are right. The role of Cassandra is a frustrating one, and if your world is to crumble to pieces around you it will be the feeblest of consolations to be able to say, 'I told them this would happen, but they wouldn't listen.' Truth, justice, beauty, wisdom may all be arrayed in splendour behind your banner, but they can act through you alone; they will remain unseen, unheard, impotent unless you enable them to fight.

You *must* be able to convince the decision-makers that you are right, whoever the decision-makers may be. You may be presenting a case to a Board or committee; you may be explaining a process to a group of trainees or to a single student; you may be describing to a group of house-wives the ingenious processes by which industries which had the problem of disposing of a highly poisonous waste-product – fluoride – induced water authorities to add it to water supplies as a compulsory medication. You may have the hardest task of all, that of trying to persuade the bad type of specialist to raise his eyes from his preoccupation with the vein of a leaf and contemplate instead the branch or even the tree. In all these situations, your audience must understand and accept; you must carry conviction. And to do this you need to become skilled in the arts of persuasion, of rhetoric, of selling.

'Black Arts', 'despicable arts', you may say. It is sadly true that during the last century evil or misguided men have more and more prostituted persuasion, rhetoric, sell-ing. The very phrase 'technique of persuasion' has un-pleasant associations with 1984, with broken men confess-ing to political 'crimes', with subliminal advertising and with psychogenic drugs. 'Rhetoric', in the Western world at least, has become a pejorative term. 'Selling' has for many people an aura of quackery, of deception, typified by the unkind story of the man whose friend asked him what sort of a job he had. Looking cautiously around he whispered, 'I work in an advertising agency – but please don't tell my mother; she thinks I play the piano in a brothel'.

The fate of the word 'rhetoric' is instructive. Once it was defined as 'the art which draws men's hearts to the love of true knowledge'. Now however the *Concise Oxford Dic-*

10

tionary entry includes 'language designed to persuade or impress (often with implication of insincerity, exaggeration, etc.)'; *Webster's New World* parallels this with its 'artificial eloquence'. This is the sense in which Disraeli used the term in 1878, when he described his sactimonious rival, Gladstone, as 'a sophisticated rhetorician inebriated with the exuberance of his own verbosity'. Nowadays rhetoric is equated with humbug.

The vital arts of persuasion have been abused, are being abused and will be even more abused : and this is why we must study to use them correctly. The battle for the mind is too important to be abandoned in a spirit of Pharisaism. The answer to lies should be truth, not just a disapproving silence.

> Matilda told such dreadful lies
> It made one gasp and stretch one's eyes;
> Her aunt, who, from her earliest youth,
> Had kept a strict regard for truth,
> Attempted to believe Matilda;
> The effort very nearly killed her.

We must not abandon the field to the Matildas, numerous and vocal though they are. Instead we must fight back with truth, *effectively*.

The vital element in presenting truth is *effectiveness*. It is not enough to be right. You must *convince* the decision-makers, convince them in the teeth of competition, competition which may be utterly ruthless. A highly-paid press agent in the United States, Edward L. Bernays, advocated a policy for promoting fluoridation in these terms :

'The conscious and intelligent manipulation of the organized habits and opinions of the masses must be done by experts, the public relations counsels; they are the invisible

11

rulers who control the destinies of millions. . . . Indoctrination must be subtle. It should be worked into the everyday life of the people – 24 hours a day in hundreds of ways. Public Health Officers cannot afford the professional modesty professed by physicians. A redefinition of ethics is necessary . . . and the subject matter of the propaganda need not necessarily be true.'
(Quoted in *Fluoridation*, The London Anti-Fluoridation Campaign, 36 Station Road, Thames Ditton, Surrey, England)

Truth for some dwells at the bottom of a well, and they lose no time in filling the well-shaft with rubble and muck. Truth is great, but Coventry Patmore warned of the disappointment awaiting those who trust in its unaided triumph :

> The truth is great and shall prevail
> When none cares whether it prevail or not
> > (*The Unknown Eros*)

You may feel that these warnings are overdone. If you do feel this, pause now to think about some of the decisions you have encountered in your life – decisions made by your employers, or by the armed forces, or by local authorities, or by experts of one kind or another. Have you never said to yourself, 'What on earth can they have been thinking about to come to a decision like that?' or more simply, 'They must be mad'? You should have little difficulty in finding examples, for the history of nations, of organizations, of individuals shows too often how easy it is for untruth to flourish, for the worse to appear the better case.

The World War of 1939-45 provides a disturbing

example of the powerlessness of truth, of the weakness of mere evidence. In that war Professor Lindemann, or Lord Cherwell as he later became, played a large part in directing the British nation's scientific effort. Tizard, a man of equal or higher ability, played a minor role. In his book *Science and Government,* C. P. Snow described a key conflict between the two men, when the very important question of the strategic bombing of Germany was being studied. Lindemann enthusiastically advocated this form of warfare and produced a cabinet paper supporting his views.

'The paper went to Tizard. He studied the statistics. He came to the conclusion, quite impregnably, that Lindemann's estimate of the number of houses that could possibly be destroyed was five times too high.

'The paper went to Blackett. Independently he studied the statistics. He came to the conclusion, also quite impregnably, that Lindemann's estimate was six times too high.

'I do not think that, in secret politics, I have ever seen a minority view so unpopular. Bombing had become a matter of faith. I sometimes used to wonder whether my administrative colleagues, who were clever and detached and normally the least likely group of men to be swept away by any faith, would have acquiesced in this one, as on the whole they did, if they had had even an elementary knowledge of statistics. In private we made the bitter jokes of a losing side. "There are the Fermi-Dirac statistics," we said. "The Einstein-Bose statistics. And the new Cherwell nonquantitative statistics." And we told stories of a man who added up two and two and made four. "He is not to be trusted," the Air Ministry then said. "He has been talking to Tizard and Blackett."

13

'The Air Ministry fell in behind the Lindemann paper. The minority view was not only defeated, but squashed. The atmosphere was more hysterical than is usual in English official life; it had the faint but just perceptible smell of a witch hunt. Tizard was actually called a defeatist. Strategic bombing, according to the Lindemann policy, was put into action with every effort the country could make.

'The ultimate result is well known. Tizard had calculated that Lindemann's estimate was five times too high. Blackett had put it at six times too high. The bombing survey after the war revealed that it had been ten times too high.'

Rival presentations of fact and opinion may result in wrong decisions: it is impossible in this imperfect world that this should not happen sometimes. But this cannot be an argument for *not* putting forward one's case as powerfully as possible. One of the major international crimes of the twentieth century, the establishment of the Zionist state of Israel in Arab Palestine, came about at least in part because the decision-makers heard one side of the case, and one side only. Dr John Davies, for many years Commissioner-General of UNWRA (United Nations Relief and Works Agency for Palestine Refugees in the Near East), underlined the importance of this in his comments on Zionist activity in the USA from 1942 onwards:

'they succeeded . . . in getting resolutions passed in both the House of Representatives and the Senate, calling for the United States to use its good offices to open Palestine for immigration and to establish a Jewish Home there. In addition, they inspired scores of public statements by mayors and governors, and by prominent businessmen, entertainers, editors, professors and churchmen, urging a similar course.

'A large proportion of the world, including the Western world, knew little about modern Palestine or the struggle that had been taking place there over the immigration of Jews and efforts to found a Jewish State. In so far as the American public was concerned, most people had never heard the Arab side presented. The result was a widespread acceptance of the Zionist point of view. Not only that, but the public, Gentile as well as Jewish, responded generously to Zionist appeals for funds to finance their programme.' (John H. Davis, *The Evasive Peace* : John Murray, 1968)

Once a falsehood has been established, once a wrong policy has been put into operation, once a way of thinking has become habitual, the task of correcting is hard indeed. Truth is always slow to overtake the lie. Thus it is that even the more absurd pronouncements of pinky self-styled 'progressives' gain a hearing and exercise influence. Thus it is that most Britishers probably believe that there has been a significant continuing Jewish presence in Palestine since Biblical times : in reality even as late as 1922 there were only some 84,000 Jews in Palestine. Thus it is that most USA citizens accept that to be anti-Israeli is to be anti-Jewish, which is as if to be anti-Nazi is to be anti-German.

As in international affairs, so in national : it is terrifyingly easy for a glib charlatan to outdo an honest but inarticulate rival in popular appeal. 'All the people' can be fooled for too much of the time. Some successful practitioners hold that the bigger the lie, the better. It was Adolf Hitler who declared : 'The great masses of the people . . . will more easily fall victims to a great lie than to a small one.'

15

As we endure whatever follies mankind has in store for itself during the rest of the twentieth century, it seems likely that Lindemann versus Tizard, Zionism versus Palestine, specialist in Subject X versus specialist in Subject Y type situations will become more common. Those who make decisions are not, and cannot be, experts in all the subjects which ought to weigh in their decision-making. At the lower end of the scale we have people deciding at the polling booths who shall govern their country; at the other extreme we have highly intelligent managers choosing between rival policies on marketing, research, or investment. Both situations contain the danger that decisions are made not in accordance with facts but in accordance with the effectiveness of the rival presentations of the facts.

The increasing fragmentation of knowledge is one of the greatest sources of hazard. As specialists become more narrow and their subjects more esoteric, the risk increases that the man with a good idea will lose to the man with the inferior idea. Unless the quality of presentation matches the quality of the idea, a Gresham's Law of Demagoguery will apply. Short-term, the race will be to the glib; long-term, as Lord Keynes remarked, we shall all be dead! Specialization helps to create the conditions for death through second-best decisions, a danger which many students of Systems Theory have foreseen. Professor Kenneth Boulding sees the associated peril, that specialists will not be able to communicate at all outside their own narrow realms :

'Hence physicists only talk to physicists, economists to economists – worse still, nuclear physicists talk only to nuclear physicists and econometricians to econometricians. One wonders sometimes if science will not grind to a stop in an assemblage of walled-in hermits, each mumbling to himself words in a private language only he can understand.' (Kenneth Boulding: *General System Theory*, Management Science, April 1956)

This is no remote academic fear. In our work of training Research Scientists to communicate we, the authors, often deal with groups of a dozen men and women from the same laboratory or complex of laboratories. Although their specializations differ, these people need to communicate with each other because they work on different aspects of the same problem; at any time they may have to collaborate closely. As a rough check on the extent to which members might have difficulties in understanding each other, we often do a simple exercise.

This is what happens. Each member writes down about ten technical or specialist words and phrases that he would be most reluctant to do without – expressions he uses very often in work. A medical practitioner for instance would probably include terms like syndrome and antibiotic. Each member then reads out his list and as he does so his colleagues individually put each term under one of four headings. If a member understands a term completely, is perfectly sure about this, would be prepared to explain it to the Royal Society in full conclave, he makes a mark in 'Column 100 per cent'. If he is fairly happy with a term it goes in the 'More or less OK' column. A word or phrase which conveys only a general meaning goes into 'Dubious'; anything that produces the reaction 'No, I don't get that at all, really' goes into the column headed 'Lost'.

One such exercise with twelve research scientists produced these totals, which are typical of many other groups:

Understanding of Colleagues' Specialist Vocabulary

100 per cent	More or less OK	Dubious	Lost
602	375	147	76

The exact figures do not matter. What does matter is that nearly a fifth of the commonest terms used in a group of specialists working closely together were judged obscure by the group members themselves. Later exercises during training usually show that members are too optimistic in their assessments.

Lack of understanding between specialists of different tribes, or between specialists and laymen, is not the sole hindrance to presenting information effectively. An organism depends for its health on having a free flow of accurate and timely information about its own internal operations and about what is going on around it; so does an organization. An inefficient communication channel, whether between limb and spinal cord or between Company Division and Company Head Office, leads to poor quality working or even to collapse. This is a two-way traffic : just as the quality of information available limits the capacity of the organization to respond effectively, so the quality of the organization limits the capacity of the information channels and determines how much suppression and distortion shall exist. Some aspects of this are touched on in the companion volume to this one – *Reports and How to Write Them* – in the second part of the chapter on 'Aim'. Even in healthy organizations, increase in size and complexity will aggravate the problems of coherence and of effective communication flow. Dinosaurs provide a *memento mori* for large corporations.

The organism-organization analogy can be extended, for both are subject to malignant growths, diseases where one part of the system multiplies to the detriment of the whole. Industry and government provide numerous examples of clannishness, suspicion, empire-building. Rival groups in the same organization too often ensure that the right hand spends great amounts of time and effort in trying to stab the left hand in the back. On a larger stage many people see tumours on a national scale. In Britain for instance they point to the growth of the Civil Service; the spread of consultancy firms whose main competence lies in choosing an impressive address and producing impressive publicity for themselves; or the proliferation of low-quality scientific researchers throughout industry.

All the parts of an organization *should* behave like coherent sub-systems, uniting their efforts for the prosperity of the whole system. This is not a plea for even more organization-men with grey flannel suits and faces : co-operation and coherence do not exclude eccentricity and strong individuality. But many Boards and Cabinets resemble the body of five executive directors which was described by one of them as 'five horses all trying to pull the same chariot in five different directions'. Muddle, strikes, waste, low profitability, and take-over bids are some of the consequences of ignoring the communications problems we have been considering. No one should claim that effective communications alone will bring about a cure of organizational ills and discords; but without effective communications these evils will spread like fungus in a damp cellar.

So much for the *need* to communicate : either the man with a worthwhile message gets it through, or the more plausible rival beats him. Victory in war, the survival of a country, success in business – all depend to an important degree on information. But not only country or company

19

flourish when the right messages reach the right destinations in the right form at the right time : there are associated benefits for the originators of such messages. The man who communicates effectively has the pleasure of getting his ideas accepted and seeing those of his rivals rejected. His reputation and his income rise together.

In her charming book *It Gives Me Great Pleasure,* Emily Kimbrough confesses that, through all the vicissitudes of lecture tours, one great and inspiring ideal upholds her : she is getting paid for doing the job. Anyone who still feels reluctant to descend to the rough and tumble of the platform, the dais, the speaker's chair or lectern should realize that, where the speaking concerns his job, he too is being paid for it. If the man who should speak effectively does not make every effort to do so, then he is not doing what he is paid to do. Stafford Beer made an important point in 1959 when he was Head of the Department of Operational Research and Cybernetics, United Steel Companies Ltd. He was considering the qualities required in a scientist who was about to switch from the laboratory to O.R. (Operational Research); but the Lindemann-Tizard episode indicates that Beer's words apply elsewhere with equal force. Beer wrote :

'The man must be highly intelligent, a thinker. Unfortunately many such people are shy and inarticulate. But the O.R. man should express himself with ease and fluency, projecting his personality and ideas like a politician. He needs considerable strength of character too, for ertswhile specialist colleagues may scorn him for leaving the laboratory, while his new managerial friends may resent quite bitterly the help he is trying to give. Finally, although he is a dispassionate objective scientist, he may have to produce

the vehemence of a salesman in defence of the product –
his results. It is a true but most awesome platitude that if
an O.R. man cannot "sell" his conclusions then he might
just as well not have come.' (Stafford Beer : *Operational
Research and Personnel Management,* Institute of Personnel Management, 1959)

And if the man 'might just as well not have come' then
he might just as well not be paid.

By now you may agree that rhetoric (in its old good
sense), selling, persuasion matter, and that you should become more expert in these arts. But can a mere book help
you to improve? Surely speaking must be practised in
public just as sailing must be done on water?

To some extent it is true that practical experience is
necessary. No one becomes a second Sir Winston Churchill
or a Sir Francis Chichester by reading solely, and nothing
can replace expert on-the-spot coaching. But this book can
help you to gain more from any coaching you may receive.
It can help you to prepare your talks so that the pains of
speaking are reduced and your effectiveness increases. This
book can also help you to avoid faults so that, in time, even
without the help of expert on-the-spot criticism of your
performance, you can learn to improve your technique of
self-expression.

Neither effective speaking nor effective sailing 'comes
natural'. Most of us have been subjected to the influence
of so many awful examples among schoolmasters, clergy,
lecturers and politicians that even if speaking well did
'come natural' in the state of innocence, it no longer does
so. No improvement will come unless you are prepared to
work hard, to prepare thoroughly, to observe yourself intelligently. Those who believe that all they need is Alfred

21

Jingle's 'the gift of the gab' are likely to end in trouble : Jingle himself nearly died as a poor debtor in the old Fleet Prison! Gabsters are unlikely to suffer such a fate, unfortunately perhaps, for many of them could be spared. But they are pretty certain to end up metaphorically where the young Jerome K. Jerome and another boy ended up literally. The two lads decided that sailing needed neither experience nor preparation – just wind; they put their theory to the test on a good blustery day and ended up dismasted and aground on a mud bank.

II

The Plan of This Book

Where are you going to, my pretty maid?

You do the most important work of a speech before you open your mouth. This is the preparation, when you have to get clear in your own mind just what you hope to achieve and what characteristics of your audience and environment will help or hamper you. So we examine aim and preparation first.

Many people use a laborious and inefficient way of preparing to talk. It is hardly too much to say that they set themselves a task that only a small minority could achieve : this is the task of writing out a speech and trying to learn it by heart. We provide a less troublesome method of preparing which will help you to talk confidently and well.

The most worrying part of a speech for many people is the actual delivery. We therefore examine what you can do to make standing up and speaking less of a burden for you, and less of a strain for the sympathetic members of your audience. We look at the role of language and discuss why some speakers seem to think that to use the more indigestible words of a dictionary is the way to influence an audience. We then suggest how you can deal with the problems of nervousness; how you should use your voice; how you can make sure that you and your listeners make and keep contact as you speak. We also discuss the most fruitful way of dealing with questions.

Next comes an *à la carte* chapter dealing with four special problems. These are case presentation; social speaking; what to do – other than run – when you are suddenly asked to 'say a few words'; and how to get some value out of 'reading a paper'.

The last chapter, 'Make Sure You Improve', indicates some of the things you can do, either alone or in co-operation with others, to make yourself more constructively self critical, more aware of your own habits of preparation and of presentation, and of where they need amendment. Books and trainers can give advice : only you can apply it.

III

Your Aim

'Naturally the fundamental objective of any business is to make a profit and to increase it. But it is necessary to be much more specific. Each company must decide just how, in view of the resources and talents available to it, it can best carve out its own profit-making niche in the economy. For example, some companies plan to attract customers by producing particularly high-quality products at premium prices for a selected group of customers. Others aim to serve a clientele that's primarily interested in low prices. Either may be a good objective, depending on the company's circumstances.'
Ernest Dale & L. C. Michelon: *Modern Management Methods*

'The manager has a specific tool: information. He does not "handle" people; he motivates, guides, organizes people to do their work. His tool—his only tool—is the spoken or written word or the language of numbers. No matter whether the manager's job is engineering, accounting, or selling, his effectiveness depends on his ability to listen and to read, on his ability to speak and to write.'
Peter F. Drucker: *The Practice of Management*

The first step in preparing to give a talk is to decide as clearly as you can just what the talk is meant to *do*. What information do you want to convey? What effect do you want that information to have? Will you be satisfied to leave a general impression of your theme with your audience, or do you want them to remember definite details? Do you want to change the way the audience behave, and, if so, how realistic is your aim, with this group, in the time available?

These are difficult questions, but if you fail to do your best to answer them neither you nor your audience are likely to emerge happily from your encounter. As with many difficult questions, you will be able to cope with the *aim* problems more easily if you examine them bit by bit. The answer to any one bit of the problem may force you to adjust the whole of the rest of your approach, and this means more work for you : but you cannot hope to satisfy your audience without working.

You must ask yourself these five questions :

> WHO are my audience?
> WHAT do they already know about the subject?
> WHY are the audience listening?
> HOW can I use or overcome my audience's prejudices?
> WHERE and WHEN is the talk to be given, and HOW LONG am I allowed?

Similar questions arise when a written report is being prepared. Chapter 3 of *Reports and How to Write Them*, the companion volume to this, deals with these questions in detail. When the material of a speech is to be published as a report or paper, you would be well advised to read that chapter.

WHO are my audience?

The speaker has a harder job than the report writer. The writer can segregate his material : his summary aims at all readers, but detailed specialist material is packaged separately, and clearly identified so that readers can go

direct to the items they require. During a talk the audience
cannot execise any such selectivity – they cannot skip
sections or turn straight to the appendices; unless they go
to sleep or walk out, members of an audience are captive.
If he is to avoid passive resistance or active opposition the
speaker must think very carefully about the composition of
his audience. Will they be fairly homogeneous in interests,
knowledge of the subject, command of the language and
so on, or will the range of IQ, background and outlook be
wide? Even if the audience are wide in range, the speaker
may wish to influence certain members. For example, at
some meetings there may be a few key figures who exercise
great influence on the group, and the speaker will therefore
want to aim in particular at them.

But it is unwise to leave islands of utter incomprehension
in an audience, even if only because they can become a
disrupting influence! It is often worth making an effort to
satisfy as wide a range as possible. This comes down to
presenting a talk at two levels; you have to put the key
points over in language as plain as possible, and then
develop these key points in whatever higher level of
language you need. We return to this aspect of a talk on
page 53 where we discuss Section Transits.

People responsible for assembling audiences can do much
to help the speaker. They should take the trouble to let
the speaker know well in advance the kind of group he is
to address, the members' level of knowledge of the subject,
and their interests. The speaker has then a much greater
chance of giving a talk attuned to the audience's needs.
The secretary or chairman of a meeting should never ask
a speaker to address a meeting without this preliminary. If
secretaries and chairmen had the intelligence and courtesy
to provide this information, it would mean the end of such

hopeless briefs as 'Well, we are a very varied group, from apprentices to directors, and their interests are very wide.'

The ideal to aim at is that everyone *entitled* to be in your audience should follow you throughout the whole of your discourse. We stress 'entitled'; there is not the slightest need for the tea-lady to follow the deliberations of the committee she serves as they discuss the capital investment programme in the boardroom. There is every need for her to understand the terms of an Employee Benefit Plan when the Staff Manager explains it.

This should dispose in advance of the man who defends his utter incomprehensibility to everyone, not always excluding himself when he hears a tape recording of his talk some six months later, by saying 'You are really expecting me to explain everything to everyone in words of one syllable and it can't be done'. In fact, we aren't and it can't; but we do say : 'Explain so that the people you are *meant* to be communicating with do get the message.'

WHAT do my audience already know about the subject?
More and more people now give at least lip service to the dictum 'I cannot communicate with other people except in terms of their own experience'. But they still find it hard to realize that their expertise is a mystery to others. Some who are vaguely aware of it follow the lead of the Englishman abroad who speaks his own language louder and faster if he finds the 'ignorant natives' don't readily understand him. And, as always, it is easier to recognize that the other man is talking incomprehensibly than to accept that we ourselves are doing just this. At a recent practice speaking session for technical men from various disciplines, the man who had ten minutes earlier declared, 'Everyone knows what igneous rocks are and why they are not oil-bearing,'

was most scathing of a later speaker who rashly used the term 'bus bar' in his talk on electricity supplies!

The speaker often has a good chance of judging what his audience know; he has several sources of information :

1. Sometimes he will know his audience personally. This won't always stop him from spouting accountese or bacteriology or organic chemistry at a non-specialist meeting, but it does remove any shadow of excuse.

2. Sometimes the description of the audience gives enough clues : The Royal Society; the Science VI form; apprentices in the third year of a specified programme.

3. Sometimes the secretary or organizer can be questioned; the more specific your questions the better. The query 'What sort of people are they?' may call forth the reply 'Lousy', whereas the queries 'What is their general level of education?' or 'What is their age range?' or 'How many previous speakers have you had on this subject?' all warrant a clearer answer.

4. Occasionally the speaker can contact the audience direct. For instance, one of the authors recently sent a questionnaire to members of a management development course he was to run, asking for brief details of education, job description, management journals read.

5. If previous information is not available the audience itself can help you. In some circumstances you can question them directly. You can ask : 'What does the term X mean to you?' Or you can encourage them to ask questions during your talk. This information helps you to pitch your talk at the right level for your audience. If you do adopt this method, your preparation must be very thorough to make sure you have a wide enough range of facts and examples.

6. You can often gather information from the expressions on the faces in front of you; this will tell you if people are getting lost. Remember that people may yawn because they are exhausted as well as because they are bewildered and bored : for either you should allow a break, and probably let in some fresh air as well. With experience you will soon learn to tell from the look of an audience whether they are ahead of you, keeping up, or lost in the fog.

WHY are my audience listening?

Any talk, like any report, should answer questions : the questions the listeners would ask *if they knew enough about the subject to ask the right questions*. It is surprising how useful a tool this idea can be. It disciplines us into remembering that no audiences want to hear everything we know about a subject; it disciplines us into remembering that items which are of great significance to one audience are utterly boring to others.

There is a further advantage from asking ourselves what information will help our audience, for this may help us to realize that we do not really know what *is* relevant to other people's needs. This may make us more humble; it may make us try to find out more about their needs. If doing this helps to break down the barriers of remoteness, suspicion, ignorance and delusion that so often separate one section of an organization from another, then not only better talking will result but better running of the organization.

To sum up : the purpose of asking 'Why?' is to ensure that you provide the information your audience need; the purpose of asking 'What?' and 'Who?' is to ensure that you do not talk to the converted or to your close co-thinker only. Remember that what is fascinating to the research chemist is mostly likely to be an irrelevance to the production engineer; 'an elegant experiment' cuts no ice in the pilot plant.

HOW can I use or overcome my audience's prejudices?

People differ. The same person at different times, and different persons at the same time, will act and think very differently. In the convenient notation of the semanticists:

$$Mr\ A_{1963} \neq Mr\ A_{1973}; Mr\ A \neq Mr\ B$$

($\neq$ merely means 'is not equal to')

In fact your aim as a speaker is to make sure that:

$$Mr\ A_{before\ your\ talk} \neq Mr\ A_{after\ your\ talk}$$

You also need to make sure that the direction of change is the one you want. To achieve this change with the varying range of people in any group you have to adopt some of the salesman's techniques.

The 'pure' researcher who shrinks disdainfully from any taint of the commercial should remember that if he cannot sell his product, namely his ideas, then he will sooner or later have to yield to a more persuasive rival. The customer who has to be persuaded to do what you want may be the University Grants Committee, or a potential employer, or the Board of your own company; but that customer must be *persuaded* – you must present the facts in such a way that you convince, you make a sale.

The successful salesman and the successful speaker both allow for the non-rational elements in human beings : we

31

are feeling as well as thinking animals. People need to feel important, we need to be reassured, we need to feel that *our* interests are being looked after, we need to be treated tactfully. John Rowan Wilson gave good advice to young scientists on how to get funds for their pet projects, in a *Punch* article, 'Raising the Wind' :

'Be tactful
Remember that most scientists, even eminent ones, live in a constant fear that their life's work has been a complete waste of time. They react very emotionally to anything which could be interpreted as an attack on it. It is therefore highly inadvisable to put forward a project designed to prove that Lord Chigwell, FRS, a prominent member of the grant-giving committee, has been talking through his hat for the past forty years. An almost equally tactless approach is to find some project which is being carried out by one of your seniors at enormous expense, and suggest a way of doing the same experiment at a fraction of the cost' (*Punch,* Sept 11, 1968).

People can be surprisingly shortsighted and tactless, simply because they do not try to put themselves emotionally into the position of the people they are addressing. A word of warning : in avoiding tactlessness, be careful to avoid going to the other extreme. Untruth and its near relation, flattery, both defeat their purposes sooner or later.

Untruths are of various kinds – as Chapter I indicated. They include such things as a claim that a market survey gives an accurate picture of the buying habits of all social groups, when the sample involved is too small in some areas to be valid; a claim that a drug will not have undesirable side-effects; a claim that some new interference with our natural environment is only dangerous in the eyes of cranks; a claim that a favourite method is 'the only method'. Or claims can be downright lies, of the type used by the old patent medicine vendor and many modern politicians.

Disraeli is supposed to have said that all women like the butter of adulation, but that with Queen Victoria he laid it on with a trowel. This may be an instance of fooling one of the people all of the time, but for most people, flattery soon palls. Do not tell your audience *in so many words* that they are intelligent, or good cooks, or the most aware of any you have met, unless it happens to be true and cannot sound condescending. Instead, pay them the genuine compliment of thinking beforehand of just how your subject matter can be angled to satisfy their real requirements. Too many talks assume, as do too many negotiations, that a 'non-zero-sum-game' is not possible; that someone must 'win' and someone must 'lose'. Many speakers approach their task as if they were in competition with their audience or else trying to outwit them. Other speakers are constantly on the defensive because they are trying to force their own pet ideas, or needs, down someone else's throat. If instead, speakers asked themselves in their preparaation,

What interests, needs, and prejudices have the listeners?

What benefits does my theme offer them, how can I help them?

How can we co-operate in communicating relevant and beneficial ideas to each other?

the nervous strain of many talks would decrease and success increase.

Abstaining from flattery and untruths doesn't mean refraining from presenting your case in the best light, just so long as the light isn't moonshine. Nor does it mean: 'Be blunt and rude'. You must remember to choose your words tactfully; don't use fighting talk unless you must.

Many words have very strong emotional associations, and we should be chary of using them unless we have realized that a situation seen from our own viewpoint may be wildly different if regarded from other points of view and interest. What to you is a mere statement of fact may be taken as an attack by a person closely involved in the situation you describe. For example, you should be chary of describing an experiment as 'ill-conceived', a strike or a management statement as 'irresponsible', and expenditure as 'wasteful'. We do not say that this kind of language is never justified, but we do advise you to think well of the possible consequences before you use it.

The difference that viewpoint makes to one's feelings about a situation and to the language one uses is well illustrated by 'Conjugations for Conferees' which appeared in *The Economist* of April 13, 1963.

> I am a Great Power
> You are not
> He has delusions of grandeur
>
> I am a competitive exporter
> You are a cut-throat trader
> He is a neurotic deflationist
>
> I give aid
> You tie loans
> He leaves IOUs
>
> I am developing
> You are backward
> He is hopeless.

Occasionally you as a speaker may find yourself at the receiving end of antagonistic 'You' or even 'He' language. If this happens, try to keep your temper. However destructive and rude a questioner's phrasing may seem you will still benefit by trying to understand just what he has in mind, and why he has chosen the terms he has, before you write him off as plain awkward. If he has a problem, you should try to help. If he is just bloody-minded then you can best dispose of him by refusing to get dragged into a fight. If you keep calm, the questioner's colleagues are quite likely to deal with him for you.

WHERE and WHEN is the talk to be given, and HOW LONG am I allowed?

The 'where' is often outside the control of the speaker, so this paragraph mainly addresses those who are responsible for arranging meetings. If your speaker is a stranger, try not to leave him to find his own way in a taxiless desert to the wrong gate of a large works on a foggy wet day. When he does arrive, remember that he has internal organs and that it is often a work of charity to allow him a few minutes to relieve himself before he meets the group. Find out too whether he needs time to refer to his notes.

The speaker should make his needs clear well before he arrives, and the organizer must provide what is asked for, or else let the speaker know several days ahead of the meeting that certain items are not available. Organizer and speaker between them should clear up such questions as :

Should the speaker sit or stand?

Does he need blackboard, newsprint (large sheets of paper of blackboard size), coloured chalks or pens?

Will there be any electrical equipment – and who is to provide it? If it is the speaker's responsibility to provide equipment, the organizer should ensure that the right sort of electricity is available, and that he has adaptors for plugs.

Are there to be slides? Will a blackout be needed? (If so, there must be a shaded light at the lectern.)

Does the speaker prefer to use a microphone?

Are there any 'dead' spots in the auditorium? (Many lecture rooms and halls have their individual acoustic oddities and the speaker must be warned of these.)

Any equipment provided should be good. It may be amusing when the lectern collapses just as the speaker puts his notes on it, but it hardly makes for effective communication.

Little of the above applies to the average informal talk – but still too many regular business meetings with visiting speakers are held in noisy, smoke-filled, ill-lit rooms. Often the choice is between not hearing the speaker above the noise of machinery and traffic, or not hearing him because closed windows have so fugged the atmosphere that the audience can't stay awake. Extractor fans or air conditioning can and should solve this problem.

There remain the two time questions under this heading – when and for how long should you speak. Both questions may be settled for you in the programme laid down by the host organization, but you may be able to influence them. Try to avoid speaking during that heavy period between lunch and tea. If you are running a series of talks over some days, make the mornings long and the afternoons short – even if this means making arrangements for a special

36

additional coffee break. The reason is simple : some of your audience will eat or even drink too much for lunch, and will then sink into siesta. It is surprising how many seminar organizers make this problem worse by arranging a heavy lunch, preceded, accompanied and rounded off by alcohol, and therefore succeeded by haze.

An obvious point, once you have erred, is that you should note in your diary the time, date and place of any talk you have contracted to give. Make too a warning note in your diary, about a month before the due date, just in case you forget to prepare. When you go to the site of the talk, take with you a note of the telephone number of your contact at the host organization, just in case you are delayed. If you fail to do this, then sooner or later you will find yourself late or lost or both, in a telephone box where the directories have been destroyed by vandals, unable to get any answer from Directory Enquiries.

Now to the length of time you should talk. No pure lecture should last for more than fifty minutes and even this should have oases of relaxation in it, to enable listeners to get their second and third wind. If you intersperse your lecture with discussion then you may well hold sessions of an hour and a half or even two hours. But keep alert for signs of weariness; when they come, have a break. Get the audience to do something; let them move around and stretch their legs; give them something to work out, alone or in small groups. Don't forget that humans are body as well as mind. On many occasions, your listeners have been greeted with coffee, or have taken drinks at lunch. If their attention is diverted from brain to bladder, your eloquence will be in vain.

Whatever length of session you are allowed, do not over-run. To do so is discourteous to any following speaker, for

37

it cuts his time; it is inconsiderate to your group for it disorganizes their timetable; and it shows you up as inefficient in not planning properly. Far better to stop ten minutes early than to go on one minute too long! In any case you should leave time at the end of a talk for people to ask questions on any points that need clarifying or expanding. However carefully you prepare, you cannot hope to cover every aspect of your subject to the full satisfaction of all your listeners. So allow time at the end.

What if no one has any questions? The answer to this depends on your purpose and preferences. You can have a supplementary appendix ready to give, or you can question your group to check that they have got points which your experience warns you may have been misunderstood. Or you can just stop early.

How can you stop running over time? Partly by controlling questions – until you are well experienced it is best to leave all questions to the end. You can also help by programming your talk and deciding in advance which parts you will abandon or deal with in outline if you run short of time. You should not speed up as you find time running out nor leave it to the inspiration of the moment to decide what to pare or abandon. Decide what you will sacrifice *before* you start talking and not as you talk.

IV

Preparation

'There is gold, and a multitude of rubies; but the lips of knowledge are a precious jewel.'
Proverbs 20 : 15

'The materials to be provided depends upon the occasion, the season, and the number of persons to be provided for. The more elaborate the meal, the more difficult is the task of selecting dishes which, while they differ from one another in material appearance and flavour, will yet, when blended together, form a harmonious whole.'
Mrs Beeton's *All About Cookery*

'They that were foolish took their lamps, and took no oil, with them: But the wise took oil in their vessels with their lamps.'
St Matthew, 25 : 3-4

The great Duke of Wellington beat the French because he was a better general than Napoleon. His Grace may have been short on demagoguery, but he was good on meals and mules as well as on strategy and tactics. His preparations were thorough but not rigid; when a rope broke in his plans, he 'tied a knot' and carried on the campaign. Great managers likewise owe much of their success to careful but adaptable planning, and so do good speakers. That very experienced lecturer Phyllis Bentley wrote :

'. . . when I have given a lecture, members of the audience often come up to me and say : "What a talent for speaking you have. How lovely it must be to be able to speak so easily ! An hour without a single note !" As you will have

39

seen by now it is not "easy" at all, nor is it a special "talent", but the product of careful preparation and much hard work. I always tell these admirers so. Usually they do not believe me, but you must, if you are to succeed as a speaker.' (Phyllis Bentley : *Public Speaking*.)

It is preparation which determines whether your talk shall be chaotic or orderly; whether your audience has to rely on extra-sensory perception to follow you; whether you succeed despite yourself; or whether you and your hearers travel together in understanding even if not in agreement. If the audience are going to disagree with you, at least let them *know* what they are disagreeing with.

Preparation also decides whether your thoughts shall be fresh or stale, whether the thinking you put over is creative or dead, whether even standard material being presented for the thirtieth time remains lively or carries the odour of decay with it.

The WRONG WAY to prepare your speech

Let us first clear out of the way how *not* to prepare. Do *not* write out your speech and learn it by heart and then recite it, or try to recite it, to your audience. Or at least do *not* do this unless you satisfy four rare conditions by being : an expert script writer; a rapid learner of text (what the acting profession calls a 'quick study'); an actor of professional standard; and, finally, a prophet.

Here is why you need these four qualities.

Expert script writer
Spoken and written English differ markedly. Spoken English is less formal in its choice of words than written English. Its sentence construction is far less rigid; many of its

sentences may be grammatically incomplete, being finished with a gesture instead of with words. Spoken English makes use of changes in emphasis, speed, and tone, in a way not open to the written word. All these aspects make speech *different*.

To write in the way we talk is very difficult. If you doubt this, try this experiment. Write a description of any ordinary talk between two people discussing the weather, or a man and his wife talking about money matters, or a woman ordering things from an assistant in a shop. It is no problem to write, 'Joe walked into the restaurant, and ordered his lunch, ate it, paid for it and went out.' It is a much harder problem to fill in the episode with the words that Joe and the restaurant staff used. If Joe had to sit down and write down all the words he used to order his lunch, with all the social comments used in the process, he would never get down to eating !

Written English *sounds wrong* because it isn't what we are used to hearing. There are ceremonial occasions when a special style of language is called for, but for everyday situations the plain conversational style is best. Even if you happen to be one of the few people who can write in this conversational style, you need not waste your time doing it, since, as we show you later, it is not necessary !

One set of data must be written in detail. If you have to introduce a speaker, you must write down his name, qualifications and position. You will do well to check their accuracy with the speaker, but check or no, do *write down* those key points. Otherwise you may be reduced to the state of the chairman described by Emily Kimbrough :

'The chairman took a deep breath, reached for her hat, failed to find it, placed a tiny ball of pale blue handkerchief on the lectern, and said: "Ladies, on this happy occasion of our first meeting of the season, it is my privilege and pleasure to present" – and then she stopped. "It is my privilege and pleasure to present," she repeated, and shook out the little blue ball, applying it to her forehead and temples. When she had finished she waved the blue rag towards me in a wildly beckoning gesture. "Honey," she said, half turning to me, "you tell them who you are and what you do." With a last clutch at parliamentary form she added, "And it gives me great pleasure to present her with this opportunity of doing so." ' (Emily Kimbrough: *It Gives Me Great Pleasure.*)

Expert memory man

If you are going to read your talk you might as well give out copies and save your voice, because you will lose one of the great advantages of speaking : your immediate contact with your audience; the hints you get from their expressions; whether they seem restless or interested; whether they are nodding in agreement or frowning in disapproval. Equally important, if your eyes are on your notes the audience will lose the feeling that you are actually talking to each one of them.

So if you want to write out your address and still have the advantages of contact with your listeners, you will need to memorize your talk, for otherwise your eyes will be constantly on your script. This memorizing will waste your time and energy and you will still be worried in case you forget your lines. Even if you have memorized your script, you still need to put it across convincingly.

Actor

Few things are more painful for an audience than watching incompetent amateur actors, yet you will be one if you

42

try to deliver a prepared script. Just consider the circumstances. You will write your script at home, for example; at a certain point in your text the eye of hope will see you, the audience hanging spellbound on your lips, crashing your fist on the table and crying aloud with a voice like a trumpet some inspiring words to set men's hearts aflame. So down in your script will go the appropriate words and instructions.

But the circumstances in which you will in fact talk will certainly be quite different from those of your fancy. The table may be a worm-eaten lectern or a desk so covered with papers that it is unthumpable; your feelings will be very different from those you imagined you would have. In fact, since you lack the experience of the professional, your re-warmed enthusiasm will embarrass the audience rather than convince them.

Instead of letting your anxieties about speaking drive you into trying to become an actor, you should allow yourself to relax, and prepare your talk in the way we outline later on. Your presentation will then be natural and you will be free from the artificiality and stiffness of the amateur. You will be convincing because your gestures will express the feelings you have as you speak; they will flow from the immediate situation; they will be suitable to you as you are, instead of to you as you imagined you were going to be.

Prophet
Even if you happen to be script writer, memory man, and professional actor rolled into one, your pre-written address is still in danger unless you are also a prophet. Something may happen at the last minute to make you change your approach; a previous speaker may make one of the very

43

points you intended to make; another speaker may not turn up and you may be asked to talk for longer than planned, or an extra speaker may arrive and you may need to curtail your talk. All sorts of things can happen and unless your speaking plan is flexible, you will be in great difficulty.

A delightful example of the snags of written talks appears in Evelyn Waugh's *Scoop*. If you have not read the account of Lord Copper's speech at the dinner in honour of 'Boot of the Beast', do so for it will amuse as well as warn you. And in case you condemn *Scoop* as mere fiction, recollect that not very long ago during the formal luncheon to mark the ceremonial opening of a highly reputable British hotel, part of the ceiling fell on the assembled dignitaries. Any speaker who had references in his script to 'this outstanding example of British craftsmanship' will confirm that it is the unexpected that happens and that preparation for speeches must be flexible!

HOW to prepare your speech

The first phase of preparation we have dealt with in Chapter III – getting your aim clear. Now we look at how you can achieve that aim. There are three things to do. First, collect your material; second, select from the material; and third, organize the selected material.

Collect your material
The way you go about collecting the material can make all the difference between a pedestrian and uninspired talk and a talk which is fresh and convincing. You will hardly be speaking on subjects where your knowledge is weak. Rather, your danger may well be that you know your sub-

ject too well, for this may mean that your mind follows patterns of thought which are stale and dated. If you make up your mind too early about just what you are going to say, you are preventing it from producing fresh ideas, new thoughts, valuable new examples and so on. To plan too early in the collecting stage is to put yourself aboard the same restricted vehicle of thought as the hero of the pre-determination limerick :

> There was a young man who said Damn,
> I've just realized that I am
> A being that moves
> In predestinate grooves
> Not even a bus – I'm a tram.

Try to look at your subject afresh. It is worth noting that the advocates of drills for promoting creative thinking often get their followers to break away from the conventional way of approaching a situation. The well-known technique of 'brainstorming' follows this principle. The essence of this operation is to record all the remarks of half a dozen lively characters as they talk positively about a problem where new thinking is required. They can say anything at all, however crazy it may sound, however fantastic, for in the apparently fantastic may be concealed the germ of a really bright new idea.

Brainstorming, by the way, is not easy, and it does demand preparation. Each member should try and develop new ideas before the meeting, so that he can help to get discussion moving. If everyone waits on the inspiration of the moment the ideas which emerge will be fewer and weaker than they could be. Mutual parasitism is not a productive way of life !

Not all techniques of creative thinking are as easy to understand and accept as is brainstorming. For instance, if you have to think about the problems of paint manufacture, you may not wish to imagine yourself into feeling that you are a drop of paint rolling down a surface, frantically trying to catch hold of something to slow down your fall. You may not care to prepare to work on unbreakable glass by asking yourself which natural laws you would repeal if you could, so as to produce a substance to satisfy your needs. But some people claim to have produced fresh ideas in this kind of way. If you want details about this kind of approach you can find out more about it through reading *Synectics* by William J. J. Gordon. Be warned though; this is not a text-book on creativity; it is just one man's view of it.

Pending the development of a better way of promoting creative thinking, you can always fall back on the old but valuable method of recording your thoughts on paper freely and without any rigid plan. All you need is a block of paper and a pencil; then you just jot down whatever comes into your mind as you think about the subject of your talk. Write as swiftly as you can; don't waste time even to make sentences, but just scribble down key points of ideas that come to your mind. Use any abbreviations and private shorthand you like for making notes, as long as they will be clear when you read them later.

After some time at this jotting exercise, the ideas will come more slowly. At this point read through your jottings in a receptive, unprejudiced frame of mind. You must examine all the ideas carefully, particularly the more apparently outrageous or irrelevant ones, for these can trigger off valuable fresh ideas or remind you of something you had forgotten all about. Naturally, you must note down these additional points as soon as they occur to you. It is fatal to new ideas if you say to yourself, 'Ah, I'll remember that point', because you won't, unless you write it down as soon as it appears.

When your flow of ideas ceases you should, if possible, lay your notes aside for a day or two. This provides an incubation period during which your subconscious mind develops the themes you thought of, and produces new ideas. Then go through your notes again and bring them up to date with your current thinking.

The jottings method does not exclude the more formal collection of facts from records, reports and reference books; but there again confine yourself in the first instance to key words or phrases. Don't forget to note also the source of each item, otherwise you will waste a lot of time trying to find it again. Leave space around each entry in your notes to put in any new thoughts which may arise as your brain works on the facts you are uncovering.

Remember, do not plan or select restrictively at this stage. If you doubt whether any particular point is relevant, put it down; you can always throw it out later on, but if you fail to record it you may lose a potentially fruitful lead. Admittedly, the answers to your 'aim' questions will impose some limitations on your mind as it searches for ideas, so that in a broad sense you already have a plan. And if you have roughed out your section headings, then they too act as boundaries. But let them be flexible at this stage.

This 'semi-free association' drill is not as easy as it sounds. Some people really have to struggle to free themselves from the rigidity of a narrow or specialist background. This is often a serious problem for specialists whose training has led them to consider each item in a situation with detailed attention : they seem unable to change gear even if they agree that it would be helpful. This is sometimes associated with a slow reading speed, and again this is perhaps the result of having to pore over very solid texts and consider carefully each element. A patent specification must be read slowly, but some people apply the same deliberate speed to material which would be better skimmed. This leads us to wonder whether those slow readers who find free jotting difficult might benefit by improving their reading speed.

Generalizing rather unfairly, we have found that engineers and accountants are among the worst 'non-jotters'. Many of them put down headings on their sheet and then a few very general terms and do no more. The result, often, is a skimpy, jerky, and abysmally dull talk. Whether many accountants and engineers are rigid because of their training or went into their profession because its rigidity suited their psyches is a moot question. But it is unfortunately true that for sheer kiss-of-death talks, accountants and engineers take some beating. This is largely because they won't lower their intellectual guard; they won't write down anything which doesn't immediately appear to be relevant; they won't stand on their heads mentally. A pity, because they are not giving their creative abilities a fair chance to express themselves!

There are various ways of improving one's ability to do this jotting trick, of which one is regular practice. For example, you can write down a word and then scribble rapidly all the ideas it triggers off. If they come as words, write them down; if they come as pictures or vague feelings, describe them. But for the really chronic non-jotter even daily practice may not help much although he *may* be aided by rapid reading exercises. He *may* find it helpful to relax physically before he tries to jot and, even if that doesn't help his flow of free expression, it will certainly benefit him in many other ways, including the way he delivers his talk.

In the long term, anyone will jot more fruitfully, the wider his spread of useful information. If anyone says, restrictively, 'I am a specialist', he is unwise. He should say, 'Because I am a specialist I realize the danger of narrowness, staleness, rigidity; therefore I will try to become more aware of subjects remote from my own'.

Finally, we must recognize that getting inspiration, getting ideas, is a mysterious process and a difficult one. Anyone who imagines that doodling alone will produce good ideas in an idle empty head, will be disappointed. J. Groch puts it very well in her book *You and Your Brain* :

'Inspiration comes only to a brain which has done its "homework" – a brain which has been primed with the information needed to solve a problem and has sorted and evaluated that information. It does seem true, however, that creative ideas and new relationships are more readily discovered when the traditional techniques of thinking and of perceiving are relaxed. Freed of a conscious driver, the brain is then allowed to examine problems from a fresh angle, to juggle their components, and to experiment with more improbable but original comparisons and relationships.'

Now it may be clearer to you why such apparently irrelevant subjects as Relaxation, Semantics, and Synectics are included in the book list at the end of this volume.

Select your material

Having collected your jottings together you probably find you have ten times more material than you need. This is excellent, for it will force you to re-examine your aim, and check whether, from the fresh viewpoint which a free search in the subject has provided, you wish to amend that aim. You may decide that the aspect you had in mind to talk on is not really the best, only the one which was nearest to hand or the one you happened to think of first. You may decide that the questions you thought the audience should ask are now due to be amended.

Once you have re-established your aim, select from your jottings those items which you want to use for this particular occasion. Write them out on fresh sheets of paper or, if you prefer, write each one on a separate sheet or slip. The extra trouble is well worth taking as it makes your planning so much easier.

Even before you clarified your aim, you may well have had in mind tentative headings for your talk. This may be an invariable characteristic of our brains, that they hold available certain potential frameworks round which we can group our ideas. What matters is that during the aim and collection stages the plan shall be very lightly held, kept almost out of consciousness. It seems inevitable that, as you think about your aim and assemble your material, a plan begins to emerge in your mind; during the selection stage, this plan takes a clearer shape. While you are in the aim and jotting stages you want to prevent the planning side from becoming uppermost; during the selection stage you can let it come forward.

Organize your material
Organizing goes hand in hand with selecting. Your purpose is to array those items you have selected for your talks under headings and sub-headings so that they form a coherent story. Small items must be marshalled into related sub-sections, instead of being scattered at random. Sub-sections in turn must link into larger sections, and the whole finally

emerge as a unified picture. At this stage you have no sentences written, just a series of major and minor headings and sub-headings, with keywords under each. The purpose of these notes is quite simple. One the one hand they are to remind you during your talk of the points you want to cover and the order in which you want to cover them. On the other hand, they are the guide lines which you will give to your listeners as you begin your talk, to make sure they can follow you adequately and gather the general direction of your thoughts before they have to cope with small items of detail. These guide lines, this framework, must be given. Cigarette card knowledge, unsorted jigsaw knowledge, is of very little value. Facts and ideas only become meaningful when we see how they relate to each other; when we see how they modify or condition or undermine each other; when we see how they all fit as sub-systems into our wider system of knowledge.

There are exceptional occasions when you will want to conceal from your listeners where you plan to go. We discuss these later, on page 89 but they are exceptions. Even on those occasions, *you* need the headings as signposts to keep you on the right path.

Quite possibly, by the time you have organized your notes you could give a thoroughly competent coherent talk from your headings, sub-headings and keywords. But as an insurance against coming to grief at the points where signposting and links are vital, you can add a *few* sentences at key points.

These key points are :

Introduction
Section Transits
Concluding Section

51

The introduction

The introduction is the tone-setter and context-giver of your talk. In it you need to indicate such things as the scope of your talk; whereabouts your subject fits into a wider field; the points you are going to cover and maybe the points you intend to leave out. Negative signposts are useful if people may otherwise wait for you to discuss something which you are not going to cover. Thus, in a talk on pesticides and their dangers, people might well think that you would speak about the danger to wild life, or river pollution. If in fact you only intend to deal with the dangers to humans who come into contact with pesticides, you should say so in your introduction. Negative signposts, if any, disposed of, you should then proceed to say briefly what your headings are.

This part of your talk, the Introduction, needs great care and must get across; yet it is probably the time when you feel the least confident, least into your stride. So it is a good idea to write out the opening few sentences of your talk at any rate until you are practised enough to be able always to start confidently. The shorter your talk, the more important it is that your Introduction should succeed; in a long talk you have time to cover items in detail and make up for early omissions. In a short talk every word counts! But do not fall into the error of thinking that 'just for safety' you had better write out more than the first three or four sentences! If you do, your talks will deserve to fail.

You must decide just how you will present your headings. There is an art in concealing art. There are occasions when you may feel it a little too formal or blatant to say plainly something like, 'I propose to discuss the problems of materials control under the four following headings: first of all I shall explain the role of Materials Liaison Engineer; secondly . . .' and so on. You may wish to conceal the 'first, second, etc.' under a slight coating of 'The obvious place to begin the study is to ask ourselves what physical characteristics we can identify as common to all hibernating animals. That will lead us on to examine. . . .' The choice between the two methods is largely a matter of taste and suitability. But one thing is certain, given a choice between a bare, unadorned 'First I shall explain . . . secondly . . .' and so on, and the vague, formless, confusing opening which gives us no idea of where we are going, the bare bones approach must be preferred.

Section transits

At the end of each section of your talk you may need to have a backward-pointing signpost, summing up where you have got to. If you are dubious about your ability to recapitulate without help, then a couple of sentences can be written here. More necessary though is a link sentence to get your listeners safely across from one section to another. Too many talks are made up of separate segments with no links between them. So you must decide in your preparation how to bridge the gaps. You may write out your links; but again write not more than two or three sentences, unless you want to lose contact with your audience by reading.

You will have to pay extra attention to your planning and transits if you are preparing to talk to an audience where the levels of knowledge or intelligence or both vary widely. If you are to communicate with them all, you will have to give two talks in parallel. Your introduction to each section must be in simple terms so that everyone follows it. Then, to satisfy the informed or brighter members, you will need to go into the more detailed or difficult or specialized aspects of your subject. But do remember to say each time that you are now going into technical detail for five minutes, or however long it is. Those who do not find it possible to follow you will at least feel that you have been considerate to them – and they may well pick up more than you expect thanks to your plain-language introductions.

Concluding section

There are many kinds of ending to choose from : a conclusion in the sense of a deduction ('And so from this we conclude that so and so is true'); a summary; a striking example; a list of questions for your audience to consider; an indication of future work – anything so long as it reinforces your main theme and does not distract by diverting thought into irrelevancies. And since your ending is what your audience is going to carry away with them, or start questions from, it needs to be good. A weak ending, or worse still, a non-ending of the type, 'er well, I think that's all I want to say ... yes ... well ... thank you', is a good sales opportunity lost. So here too you can write a few sentences to ensure that you tie up neatly, instead of abandoning your voyage ten yards from the jetty !

The mechanics of note making

Your notes are the device which records your distilled thoughts, so they merit careful treatment. Here are a few tips to help you to get the best out of your notes.

Gerard Fiennes, sometime head of British Railways Eastern Region, once wrote :

'People have planned new timetables and electrification with immediate success just as others – and indeed the same people – have at other times and in other places done like-

54

wise and made hogsnortons of them. Having been responsible for both success and hogsnorton, I know the difference
between them : care and lack of care.' (*The Times*, January
24, 1968.)

The same applies to the preparation of notes; care is
essential. They must be clear, for you need to read them
at a glance; so if your longhand is not readily legible write
in script or block letters. You need to be able to pick out
the headings easily, so let them be in capitals or underlined
or made to stand out in any way that appeals to you. Lay-
out is very important; your notes should be so clearly set
out that even a man who does not speak your language
should be able to pick out your headings and sub-headings
and see which point goes where.

Your notes can help you to control your timing. If, after
some experience, you find that you tend to rush on from
section to section without enough pauses, then mark pauses
by a red line or some such signal, or else put each section
of your notes on a separate sheet. It is advisable to mark
in the margin of your notes the timetable you plan to follow,
and if you are at all doubtful about your time sense, it is
vital to do this.

You should also mark which items you will omit or use
only in skeleton form, should time run short. These must
be towards the end of each section or towards the end of
your talk, since until then you will not be really well aware
of just how long you are going to take.

The notes are best made on thick paper that will not
flutter about or get too easily dog-eared. Index cards are
ideal, they slip easily into your pocket and they are neat
and easy to handle. If you use more than one sheet or
card, do number them clearly and do *not* write on both

sides. When dealing with your notes you need belt, braces and safety pins!

You may want to quote the exact words of a document; if it is just a matter of a few lines you will probably copy the item on a separate sheet and cross-reference the sheet to your master notes. If your piece of text is large, you may prefer to use a photo-copy which again must be cross-referenced to your notes. If you bring with you the original volume and read from it, be very careful. Mark each quotation point in your book with a strong slip of paper. On the slip put a reference to the point in the master notes at which you plan to use the quotation; also write the volume, title, page and paragraph number on the mark slip. On the master notes similarly show the book title, volume, page and paragraph numbers. Your audience has come to hear you, not to watch you leaf through several volumes and hunt up and down a page to find a lost reference. You owe it to their time and to your peace of mind to have your reference recall system as fool-proof as possible. This may sounds laborious but it means that even if you drop your notes or your books, you can make good without wasting time.

You may have to give a talk in a foreign language. Unless you are really fluent, your notes will probably need to be rather fuller than if you were going to speak in your native tongue. Fluent or not, you should prepare your notes in the language of the talk. This gives you a useful vocabulary check and helps you to speak without having to hunt for keywords. If you realize during your preparation that the vocabulary problem is going to be too hard for you, your remedy is not to give a talk. Instead, write a paper, give it to your audience (in advance if possible) and then have a question and answer session.

Once you have prepared your notes you will have to work hard during your talk to make yourself use them. This may sound odd, but it is surprisingly easy to slip away from one's intention and get lost in side issues generated not even by your audience but by yourself! Good workmanlike notes reduce the risk of this, and help you to keep to your plan.

V

Presenting Your Talk

'Pleasant words are as an honeycomb,
Sweet to the soul and health to the bones.'
Proverbs 16 : 24

'Jargon appeals to the illiterate, plain English to the wise. Any fool
can make things sound complicated, it is a clever speaker whose
audience all understand the talk.'
Suggestions for Speakers, Institute of Biology Journal, May 1965

'It is impossible to doubt whatever is spoken in a voice that
resembles a five-stringed-lute touched by a seraph's hand in an
enchanted garden at evening.'
Ernest Bramah: *Kai Lung Beneath The Mulberry Tree*

At the end of the last chapter you may have said: 'This
is all very well but how can I speak from mere notes? I'll
dry up, run out of words.' In practice this doesn't happen.
Over the last twelve years the authors of this book have
taught this method of speaking from notes to hundreds of
people and have sat through thousands of exercise talks.
As in any conversation, people occasionally can't think of
the exact word they want, but that is no more important
in a talk than in a conversation. The solution is to treat the
gap exactly as you would if you were chatting with friends –
be natural about it. Do the same thing as you would then.
Say: 'I can't just think of the word I want here but it is

something like——' You can even explain the whole idea and invite the audience to supply the word. Nearly always some member of the audience can help you, and at the very least, the meaning gets across. The purpose of a talk is to get ideas across rather than to pretend to be omniscient, so no one should feel that they lose face by calling on the co-operation of the audience in this way.

Even when people are no longer worried by the fear of not finding the right word, their speaking may still be hampered because they cling to false notions about the nature of a talk and the kind of language it calls for.

The Nature of a Talk and its Language

'Oh, well, in my job I sometimes have to make speeches, so I've collected a few useful words such as "necessarily" and "counsels" and "erratic" and "influential" and "trends". You'd be surprised how often you can bring them in.' (Gladys Mitchell, *Pageant of Murder*.)

A talk, a speech, is natural; there is nothing odd about it, and you do *not* need a special 'public speaking' vocabulary. There are, in fact, only two differences between a formal talk and a casual conversation. Everyone joins in a casual conversation when they feel like it, and frequently several people find themselves talking at the same time. In a formal talk only one person speaks at a time. At question time also only one person should speak at a time, and the others should listen while they wait their turn. The second difference is that in a casual conversation, no clear theme develops. Talk jumps from the pollution of rivers by sewage to the interesting fact that every post-war Socialist Prime Minister of the United Kingdom has devalued the pound sterling, then jumps off to a query about the weather or

59

the winner of the 3.30 race or the current length of female skirts. Admittedly some formal talks seem to follow this chaotic course, but they shouldn't.

The whole point about a formal talk is that the speaker should know what points he wants to make and the order in which he wants to make them. *Provided that he knows his subject* he will no more falter for words in which to present his ideas, than will a housewife who wants to tell a barrow-boy just what she thinks about the antique and mildewed tomatoes he tried to sell her from the back of the stall. If the speaker does not know the subject he should not talk on it. No one should speak unless what he says is based on a mass of supporting material. The knowledge on which a talk is based should be like an iceberg, seven-eights of which is out of sight but supporting the top. If he does know his subject he can and *should* talk about it plainly and naturally.

One way to check whether someone does really know his subject is to see how simply and naturally he can put it. The one who is unsure often conceals, or to the knowing listener reveals, his uncertainty by a barrage of would-be impressive terms. The unsureness may be psychological, or based on the knowledge that his grasp of the subject is not really strong enough to stand up to challenge. The result is often the same. Words are used to impress rather than to express; words are used to proclaim, 'I am an expert', with the implied rider, 'so you mustn't query me'; or, 'I am learned', with the same rider; or, 'I am a big man so you had not better try anything', or, 'I have magic powers of knowledge, hear my incantation, bow down and obey'. Anyone who runs speaking courses for scientists has probably noticed that the man who comes in wearing his white laboratory coat often turns out to be a bad speaker, whose language is solid with specialist jargon. The white coat and the jargon are both protective devices.

Not only the insecure scientist uses unnecessary jargon to impress his audience; anyone who feels nervous about speaking, or suspects that his educational standard is lower than that of his colleagues, tends to emit a protective smoke screen of high-flown language. For example, the water closet becomes a 'comfort facility'; the temporary typist becomes a 'typist employee on a temporary basis'; the office boy almost becomes 'the junior member of the administrative-functions lower-echelon direct labour force'. The man who, over a glass of beer, 'goes home', 'proceeds in a homeward direction'; things don't happen, they 'eventuate'. 'I'm sorry, I don't get that' descends into 'I regret that as at present advised I am not fully seized of the significance of that comment'. 'We try to use' blows up into 'we endeavour to utilize'.

This pompous longwinded language is as futile as the commercialese clichés which still clutter up the letters of some of the mustier decaying companies. Don't use it. Say what you mean as directly and plainly as you can : use no words that would sound odd it you were talking about your subject in the bar of a public house. Inflated language may impress a few of the more stupid members of an audience; the others may be mildly amused at first, but will soon become irritated. Don't be misled by the advice which Bunthorne offered in Gilbert and Sullivan's *Patience* :

> If you're anxious for to shine in the high aesthetic line
> as a man of culture rare,
> You must get up all the germs of the transcendental
> terms, and plant them everywhere.
> You must lie upon the daisies and discourse in novel
> phrases of your complicated state of mind,

61

The meaning doesn't matter if it's only idle chatter of a
transcendental kind.

And everyone will say,
As you walk your mystic way,
'If this young man expresses himself in terms too deep
for *me*,
Why, what a very singularly deep young man this deep
young man must be !'

Nowadays listeners are liable to replace the word 'deep'
by 'dense'.

This does not mean that only short, everyday words
should be used in speech. Technical terms *must* be used
for the sake of accuracy and speed of communication, but
only when they are fully understood by the audience.
'Prophylaxis is to be preferred to therapy' should *not* replace 'Prevention is better than cure', unless the former will
convey a more accurate message to the particular audience.

Typical of the ignorance that lurks in the gloom behind
abstruse terminology is the experience of a physicist in a
speech practice group, who decided to explain multi-valued
algebra to a mixed audience, including medicos and economists. He began in good style but stopped after five minutes,
and when told, 'That's fine, go on,' said, 'I can't. Now I've
tried to explain this simply to you people, I find I don't
know nearly as much about it as I thought I did'. He was
a wise enough man to call his own linguistic bluff, and was
thereafter better placed to know where his knowledge was
weak. Many people will defend themselves against plain
speaking by saying, 'Oh, but it's so unprofessional', or, 'It's
undignified', or 'People will think I am stupid'. People who
react like this are rationalizing, concealing their fears. Let
them instead restrict their talks to subjects they know, pre-

pare fully and talk plainly; then some at least of their fears will evaporate like magic.

As with many other aspects of successful speaking, it is a long task to get one's language direct and simple. To do so may involve doing some hard study on the part language habits play in our thinking. It may lead into the disturbing paths of semantics; for some it may only be possible after they have examined why they use the kind of language they do and, in the USA phrase, 'what are they trying to prove,' and to whom. It is possible that no really insecure person can communicate simply. Anyone who wants to think more about these matters can get a start from the books listed at the end of this volume under the heading 'Language and Thinking'.

The place of humour

The dull-minded tend to fear and mistrust anything that is not stodgy and pedestrian, but you must not let them control you. Occasional light relief is positively helpful if it reinforces a point you are making, or reduces tension and helps you to get people into an open frame of mind, or just gives everyone a mental breather during what would otherwise be an overlong mental effort. The time span during which people can really give full attention to a speaker is remarkably short. Even twenty minutes without some sort of let-up is a heavy stint.

You can often overcome the hostility of those characters who feel that whimsical equals wicked and flippant equals shallow, by explaining to them that they will get on further and better if you occasionally use the tool of humour to carve out a rest pause for them. But do make sure your humour is not offensive. Jokes about psychological or physiological defects, for instance, should be barred. Your humour must always be relevant to your subject. It should emerge *naturally* from what you are saying, not be forced in as a deliberate exercise in funniness. There are few things more distracting than the irrelevant joke. The light relief in your talk should be used in the way Anthony Trollope's well-dressed Mrs Stanhope used ornament – not as an end in itself but as a reinforcement or highlighting of an underlying theme :

'She was rich in apparel, but not bedizened with finery; her ornaments were costly, rare, and such as could not fail to attract notice, but they did not look as though worn with that purpose. She knew well the great architectural secret of decorating her constructions, and never descended to construct a decoration.'

Personal points

Good preparation, and the determination to call a spade a spade unless you really ought to call it 'an agricultural implement designed for . . .' go a long way towards making you a good speaker. There are still, however, various points of technique which can help or mar your talk, however good your language, however careful your choice of material.

There are three main factors :

> Nerves and Mannerisms
> Speed and Voice
> Awareness of your Audience

The most worrying is nerves so let's take that first.

Nerves and Mannerisms

Nearly everyone feels nervous before having to give a talk. The feeling may range from an enjoyable awareness of being tuned up, all the way to a knee-knocking, butterflies-in-the-stomach terror. Large, tough men sometimes tremble at the thought of standing up and speaking in front of an audience.

If you are one of those who frets and fumes, do not imagine you are alone; you are in the class with many fellow sufferers. It may help to think for a moment why we do feel nervous. Since there is no physical danger in most cases, it does seem odd until we remember two things. In many circumstances our prospects may brighten or dim as a result of our talk; a sale or non-sale, promotion or by-passing may be involved. But besides this, humans rely very much on feeling that they are well regarded by their fellows. We are anxious, since our self-esteem will suffer if we fail when we are in such a conspicuous position, right in front of an audience. We see ourselves reflected in the eyes of our colleagues and fear to see our self-image dimmed.

In the short term we can often reduce nervousness by preparing carefully; or, put the other way round, if we haven't prepared we are almost bound to feel worse than if we had!

The attitude you have to your audience can help you. If you approach them as enemies to be fooled and beaten, you will probably feel more nervous than if you approach them thinking: 'How can I provide these people with the information they *really* need?' In this context it may help to remember that even with a hostile audience, sincerity and truthfulness can help to win a fair hearing. With some groups honesty even has the attraction of novelty.

Physical preparation can also help. Two or three deep breaths before you start can relax you. A good relaxed upright stance is also a counter to nerves and we suggest

65

later on that you should make a long-term study of relaxation. But even without this study you will find that you feel better when you stand on both feet, rather than twining one leg round the other; when you unclench your fists; when instead of gripping your hands tightly together you use them to add emphasis to what you are saying; when in general you unstiffen.

So much for the short-term tips on nerves. In the long-term, two interrelated themes emerge, one of which is mental and one physical.

On the mental side you may find that a fuller understanding of the way you think, and of your own psychological make-up, reduces nervousness. A word of warning however to anyone who sets out to examine his own psyche. If you start reading books on psychology you will probably find, with horror, that you have the symptoms of every mental illness you read about. Do not be unduly alarmed. We all have this experience, not surprisingly since all marked mental disorders are merely developments of tendencies which are present to some degree in all of us. A good parallel is that of reading medical dictionaries. Like Jerome K. Jerome in the opening chapter of *Three Men in a Boat*, the dipper into diseases is likely to emerge convinced that he or she has them all!

A few of the less exotic books on understanding oneself are listed at the end of this volume. One which may help you to understand others as well as yourself is Dr Berne's *Games People Play*. Unfortunately it contains much USA slang; an English language version would be a great help! But the book does provide insight into some audience behaviours which otherwise may puzzle and possibly worry speakers.

Less alarming, and probably of more immediate value,

is the physical approach to reducing nervousness. We have already said that you should adopt a relaxed stance. To the nervous speaker this may sound as if we were saying to a drowning man, 'Swim, you ass!' Well, there is some truth in this except that we are telling you to learn to swim on dry land by practising relaxation regularly, so that when you have to talk, you don't splash and splutter and sink, since you will have a skill ready for use.

Physical relaxation can benefit people physically *and* mentally. In one of the best known books on the subject, *Release from Nervous Tension,* Dr D. H. Fink writes :

'How does the practice of muscular relaxation help to cure nervousness? It is universally recognized that muscle tension is the most common symptom of nervousness. But why does the treatment of this one symptom help to cure the disease? How does proficiency in the technique of relaxation reach the cause of the disease? There can be no doubt regarding the fact that it does work. Self-direction in relaxation definitely helps in the treatment of nervousness. Results can be checked in a spirit of scientific scepticism. Since physiological relaxation cannot be harmful and actually is as beneficial as any other hygienic practice, you can try it on yourself and watch results. You can teach others and watch results. You will soon see unmotivated anxieties disappear. . . . Don't believe a word of this, but give the idea a chance by practising the technique of letting go, and see for yourself.'

Our book is not the place for an exposition of *how* to relax. Dr Fink is quite readable and his drills are easy to follow. To the nervous speaker we simply say, 'Try it and see for yourself'.

Another helpful book is *New Life through Breathing* by

William P. Knowles. As the title suggests this book is particularly valuable to those who suffer from bronchitis or asthma. But even the healthy can benefit from the simple exercises Knowles describes. Speakers will benefit directly from better breath control, and indirectly through becoming more relaxed as their whole system tones up.

Using your body

If you are relaxed, you will feel happier, and you will be able to behave more naturally than if you are tense. You will be able to emphasize your points by gesture, you will be able to make those automatic hand movements which we all use in ordinary conversation as an aid to getting our meaning over. At this point some readers will no doubt say, 'But I was told on a speaking course that I mustn't move my hands!' This strange advice *is* still being given, though the reason for it is obscure. Maybe it is thought to be un-British to gesticulate, or perhaps it is an extension of the neurosis-generating ideals of a stiff upper lip and an air of frozen calm. Whatever the reason for the fixed-hands advice, if you watch what happens to the speaker who freezes his hands you will see how mistaken the advice is. We seem to have a quantum of gestures programmed into us, and if they are barred from their natural outlet they will find another. A squirrel in a cage works off his programme of movements by running on a treadmill. The immobile speaker diverts his gesture programme of movement into nods and jerks of the head or into some other tic-like activity.

No speaker wants to give the impression that he is doing Swedish drill, or playing at windmills, or rehearsing for a melodrama as he speaks. But clear, firm, deliberate gestures are a help to an audience, not a hindrance. 'Clear, firm and deliberate' notice. Avoid fussy fumbling fiddling movements. If you want to indicate something with your hands, do it plainly in full view. Don't do a sort of coy thumb-twiddling with hands half-hidden by your notes.

As with hands, so with feet. By all means use them, but with sense. You will distract your listeners if you parade up and down like a zoo lion waiting for feeding time, but there is no reason why you shouldn't move about from time to time. If it's *natural*, do it!

Do your best to move smoothly rather than jerkily. If you suffer from disc trouble you should take particular care to avoid jerky head movements. The Cyriax physiotherapist Edith Hearn points out the danger of these in her book *You are as Young as Your Spine* :

'Since the joints at the top of the spine are small and comparatively fragile, even moderate compression may increase disc trouble. Talking vigorously with the head is rather like hitting a wooden hammer on half a dozen prune stones piled one on top of another. Learn to use the head smoothly and, if you must gesticulate, use your hands.'

The advocates of the frozen Red Indian school of speaking do have a point. *If* the choice were between immobility and a series of nervous tricks, immobility would be preferable. But the choice is not between these two evils : it is between a natural relaxed way of using your body and an irritating distracting way. If you are tense you *may* remain like a rabbit in front of a weasel : but your tension is far more likely to express itself in ways which hinder your communication, in irritating mannerisms.

Irritating mannerisms
The range of irritants is wide but they all lead to the same undesirable result : they distract attention from your mes-

69

sage so that people begin to watch your tricks instead of trying to absorb your ideas.

The unrelaxed speaker is more likely to slip into irritating tricks than is the relaxed one. But however relaxed and natural a speaker is, he still may slip into a mannerism which hinders him. He may well have annoying habits in ordinary conversation, and carry them over into more formal talks.

We deal now with a few of the more common faults. You should try and check on yourself; but if possible, ask a friend in your audience to watch for them, even when you have become an experienced speaker with plenty of practice at observing yourself.

A surprisingly large number of people do not stand firmly on both feet, nor do they stand straight. They twine one leg round another; they bend over the table in a way which hinders voice production; they grasp the table or press down on it as if it were the sole reality in a phantasmic nightmare. Others shove their hands deep into their pockets; this feels comfortable but irritates some listeners, striking them as rude, and disturbing everyone if it leads the speaker to rattle his coins and keys. Since all these things not only distract or irritate your listeners but also make you appear less than confident, your image suffers as well as your message.

Instead of leaning heavily on the table, or imitating the Tower of Pisa, stand upright, not rigidly stiff, but just naturally. You need not keep your weight equally on both feet, particularly if this leads you to sway while speaking : instead you can shift your weight occasionally from one leg to the other. Rest your hands *lightly* on the table if you like, or hold them *lightly* clasped in front or behind your back, from where they will be ready to come into play to emphasize points or demonstrate sizes and indicate shapes.

Body movements must be controlled. They can be natural and useful, or they can be a nuisance. We have already asked you to use your hands and to move about occasionally if you want. But do try to *control* what you do. Some speakers sway back and forth all the time they are on their feet; some do gymnastics with the chair. Dress gestures are common : women sometimes step out of their shoes without conscious intent, thus appearing disconcertingly to shrink; men play with their ties. Some fiddle with cigarettes or toss and catch pieces of chalk. Please don't fiddle ! Relax, and ask your friend in the audience, or the chairman, to tell you afterwards whether you slipped into annoying mannerisms.

Many speakers punctuate their talk with 'ers', 'erms', 'ahs', and such-like noises. One or two are harmless but addicts sometimes produce up to a dozen or more a minute. Often they come because the speaker is going too fast and has a morbid fear of remaining silent while he gathers his thoughts. The remedy is to slow down.

Pet phrases are another trap for the unwary. Some speakers end nearly every sentence with 'do you see what I mean?' or 'as it were' or 'O.K?' or 'you know'. There are hosts of these personal clichés and like the 'ers' and 'ahs', they distract so that people may even start counting them instead of attending to your message. A tape recorder or a candid friend in the audience can make you aware of your particular verbal mannerism.

Speed and voice

Just as mannerisms are influenced by nerves, so are speed and voice. One of the symptoms of nervousness is excessive

71

speed of talking. Unfortunately, the worst nervous period for most speakers is the opening of their address. They have not had time to warm themselves into a relaxed state, so they rush away at a colossal speed, and tear across territory where they should travel firmly and leisurely.

There are several reasons why the introduction to your speech should not be rushed. It is the time when the speaker has to learn to adjust his voice to the room; it is the time when the audience have to adjust to the speaker's voice and perhaps tune in to his accent as well. But above all it is the time when, as we pointed out on page 52, the speaker prepares the audience to receive the information that the body of his talk will present. The introduction should normally tell us plainly and directly where we are going and the way the subject is to be tackled. It should provide a guide in case we get lost, or let our attention wander, later on. If this vital material is gabbled through, then the whole key to the talk may be lost. So go *slowly* through your introduction. You will have written out the opening two or three sentences, but read them deliberately, not at the gallop.

Speed is a problem too during the body of a talk. More people go too fast than go too slow, but only a tape recorder or the comments of an observer in the audience can tell you if you have either of these faults. Over one thing you should be particularly careful : *pause* at the end of each section of your talk. This will help your audience, for it will give them a moment to absorb what you have said before they have to deal with the next stage. It will help you too, for it gives you a chance to check your notes and remind yourself of what you want to say in the next section. Again the best guide here is the critic in your audience. If you do find that you are bad at pausing, if you rush on, then remember the two tricks we mentioned on page 55. Put a thick line or some such mark in red at the end of each section to remind you to pause; and put your notes for each section on a separate card, so that you have to move to another card before you can start on the next point.

Remember in dealing with figures that numbers are very meaty material. If we miss a word in a sentence the context often helps us to fill the gap, but we normally have no such help if we miss a number in a series. So when you have to produce a lot of numerical data, slow down. Often you should repeat the figures; and best of all, write them up where they can be seen as well as heard.

If you have so many figures in your talk that you cannot easily recall them from a few keywords in your notes, it is hardly likely that your group will take them in if you just *say* them, or even if you write them up. So when you find that you need very full notes to enable you to recall numerical data, ask yourself whether you need to prepare a written note to hand out to your audience.

If you have prepared details to show or to hand out, or if you write out as you go, don't rush. Give people time to read, or to take notes, before you go on to your next point.

Speed is affected by nerves, and voice is affected by both speed and nerves. Only when mannerisms and speed are under control can you make the best use of your voice. Voices are rather like physiques : heredity and early environment have a great influence on them, but we can always make good or bad use of the voice we have developed. If anyone has a voice-production problem they will certainly benefit from practising relaxation, but voice production for anyone with a speech impediment is outside the scope of this volume – the book list at the end may be of some help. Professional help is advisable.

A good tape recorder can let you know how your voice sounds : Your version of the sound of your voice, being derived from within, is quite different from the version everybody else hears. Whatever shocks your tape-recorded voice may give you, here are some hints for improvement.

First of all, open your mouth ! A surprisingly large number of people seem afraid to do this; maybe that British stiff upper lip gets in the way again? Sloppy enunciation is unpardonable, and, if you do not give your lips and jaws free play, then sloppiness will afflict your speech. If you are afraid lest your false teeth slip, either get them changed for a set that fits or use a fixative. Should you be unlucky enough to *have* to speak to a group while you are breaking in a set, your best course is to be quite frank about it and explain the position to them ! The more you take an audience into your confidence, the better it usually is.

Do not lull your audience to sleep by keeping the same tone of voice; vary the pitch of your voice and the volume. Emphasize keywords and phrases, remembering that a quiet delivery can attract attention just as well as a strong one. But use your common sense. If you speak too quietly people will have to strain to hear you, with bad results; and if you bellow too loudly this also will impede their understanding.

Many people have a trick of speaking which you should avoid. They tend to produce sudden, very quiet, very rushed phrases. Often it seems that they have a feeling : 'What I am going to say now is not strictly relevant, so I'll shoot it across in a rapid whisper'. Either it is not relevant, in which case don't say it, or it *is,* in which case say it clearly.

74

Another place where fading often occurs is the end of sentences. The voice tends to fall there, so beware of swallowing the last words of your sentences.

One final point about voice : should you worry about accent? Unless your accent is so localized that it will not be understood by your group, you need to make no attempt to lose it. You may even find some regional accent a help. Many southern English, for example, still cling to a pathetic belief that northerners, and above all, Scots, are somewhat more honest and nobly-savage than southerners!

Regional accents should not be confused with the illiterate and debased distortions of English produced by popular idols who know no better, and imitated or admired by those who confuse vulgarity and ignorance with natural worth and unspoiled insight. The accent to be maintained is that which gives to a speaker's English that local flavour which adds an interesting tang. Wensleydale, Cheshire and Cheddar are noble cheeses; they should be preserved. Yorkshire, Devonshire, Norfolk and London are all noble accents and they too should flourish. Standard English can be as insipid as standard cheese.

Awareness of your audience
Occasionally in a large group you will find people glancing uneasily or inquisitively over their shoulders to the back of the room, trying to find out what on earth the speaker is looking at. Usually he is looking at nothing, merely obeying a bad directive found in some old booklets about talking which say, 'Always address your remarks to a point *behind* the back row of your audience'.

One needs to be *audible* in the back row, but there is no reason why one should, and every reason why one shouldn't, address a non-existent row of people. To do so is to lose a

75

very valuable feature of speaking to an audience, that of being immediately aware whether the people you are trying to get through to are following you or are lost, are reasonably interested or bored, are more or less with you or against you. You gather this information by *looking* at them as you speak, which, by the way, makes it easier for your group to attend to you.

This doesn't mean you swing round like a searchlight, or ration each person, or section in a large group, to so many words. It merely means that you look at your audience as you speak, which we do anyway when we are talking to a small group in relaxed surroundings. Be fair in your distribution of attention. Do *not* concentrate all your remarks on one person, even if he or she seems to be nodding in agreement. If you are close to your group, at a Board table for example, don't overlook the people just alongside you.

If you make use of visual aids, be careful that they do not break your link with your listeners. If you are drawing on a board you have to turn your back while you write; you can sometimes help by reading out what you are writing if it is just words. But if it is a diagram, for instance, you must stand back after each stage and leave the view unimpeded as you point to the various elements you have drawn.

You can save a great deal of time, and avoid blocking the view of your group, by using newsprint paper clipped to a blackboard – this is often called a flip board. Then you can prepare your diagrams in advance and just turn to them when you need them. If you prefer to build up a diagram in front of your audience, you can still prepare in advance by drawing very lightly in pencil. This makes sure of your spacing and proportions, and prevents you from having to crowd a vital part of your diagram into the bottom few inches. During your talk all you have to do is go over your light pencil lines with coloured crayon or marker pen. So long as your guide lines are lightly done in pencil your audience won't see them and so won't find them distracting.

It is a good thing to have nothing on your newsprint, or on your blackboard, if you still have to use that out-dated device, which is not currently relevant to your talk. It is all too easy for people to go on working through a diagram when you have passed to another theme; *you* have passed, but they have stayed behind to look at the pictures!

We have already said that if you cannot remember detailed facts, such as tables of results, from a few keywords in your notes, you can hardly expect your audience to take in those facts by their ears alone. Therefore you need to prepare a chart or slides, or supply sheets to hand out. *But* once you have gone through the items you have given out, be very firm in getting people to put the sheets out of sight. You shouldn't go on talking and let people divide their attention between details of the previous item on the handout, and details of the present item which you are discussing now. If you haven't got enough photos or specimens for everyone, or if the item is too small or too complex to show to the group as a whole, you must let it circulate. If the item is relevant it deserves to be looked at carefully, so don't go on to another point until everyone has had a chance to look. If the item isn't relevant, don't show it.

You may have to be silent while the item goes round, but that will do no harm and probably will do good. Berne wrote in his *Games People Play* that to many people 'nothing is more uncomfortable than a social hiatus, a period of silent, unconstructive time when no one present can think of anything more interesting to say than "Don't you think the walls are perpendicular tonight?" ' It may be a carry-over from this situation which makes many speakers speak when

77

they should be silent, but it is a carry-over which you should reject.

Mention of silence leads to a worrying point of audience awareness; what should you do when you lose contact with your audience by forgetting whether you have yet covered a certain item? The question answers itself if you remember that your purpose in speaking should not be to show how wonderful you are, but to co-operate with your listeners in getting useful information across to them. After all it is easy to lose the thread of your talk or your place in your notes, especially if you take questions during your talk. If this happens all you need do is to ask, 'have I mentioned "x" yet?', or go back to the last relevant item you remember discussing and ask if you covered whatever item comes next. If neither you nor your group can remember then you will do no harm by going through an item, even if it *is* for the second time.

This approach to forgetting typifies the best attitude to getting information across in *real* situations – in the market place, at the technical meeting, or in the board room. You are, or should be, trying as an honest man or woman to put over material you believe in, constructively, to people who you think will find it valuable or useful. It is a *co-operative* effort, not an exercise in glibness or confidence trickery.

If your facts are well chosen and well ordered, if you have prepared your talk in the way we suggest, your material and your line of approach will speak far more eloquently than anything else. This is not to say that you should not attend to voice, audience awareness, and all the other personal points; but do *relax* and remember that the style of delivery is subsidiary to the matter.

Remembering that and having learned to relax, you will

find that on the odd occasion when your memory plays you false you may even benefit by enlisting your audience to help you to search for that elusive phrase or concept.

One last point on keeping in contact with your audience. There is no reason why you should not let them see that you are using notes. If you glance down at the end of one point to remind yourself what comes next, the pause will help your listeners to absorb what you have just said. It will not disturb them. You are more likely to lose your listeners, have their attention wander, if you glance surreptitiously at your notes, like an adolescent student whiling away time in a dull lecture by gloating over Parisian postcards. If your notes are written on good firm card you can hold them openly in your hand. If however you tend to play with them, leave them on the lectern and refer to them there.

Dealing with Questions

However carefully you plan your talk you cannot hope to deal with every detail that may be of interest to every member of your audience. Nor can you guarantee to make every point clear to everyone. So you need to allow time for questions. If you are asked to talk for an hour, allow at least ten minutes for this filling in of gaps, this re-explaining or amplification of points.

The mechanics of accepting questions is simple enough in a small group, so long as you do not allow any one questioner to hog the lot, or to make a long speech in the guise of asking a question. When you have a large assembly it is better to ask for clearly written questions, since many people are reluctant to speak in large assemblies and this tends to leave the way too open for the cranks and publicity seekers.

79

Whether you should take questions at the end only, or during your talk, depends on the kind of aim you have. On the whole, it is advisable to leave the questions to the end of the talk, or at least to the end of a section. If anyone doesn't understand a point that is vital to your argument, or doesn't grasp a technical term, then you must allow him to stop you then and there for an explanation. But other sorts of question, particularly argumentative ones, allowed during a talk, make it very difficult to control timing, and also tend to disrupt the flow of your ideas.

You can avoid some interruptions if you state clearly at the start the main points you are going to cover and how you are going to take questions. This is especially useful when you are presenting a case to a board or committee for it enables the chairman to deal with talkative members by saying, 'Our speaker has said he is coming to that in his third point, so let's wait until then'.

You must prepare for questions. This may involve bringing along with you reference files or books; or it may mean working out what queries are likely to arise, especially those that may be hostile to your view-point. If you are wise you will list the hostile questions that could be fired at you. This list may even induce you to alter your viewpoint; at least it will equip you to deal constructively with difficult questions when they do arise.

When you are answering questions do not be afraid to admit an error and, if you do not know the answer, just say so. If necessary, take time to consider your answer and defer giving it until you are ready. Try to maintain the attitude of 'we are adults doing the best we can to solve a problem in which we have some common interests'. Even if your questioner is rude – in fact, especially if he is rude – do not let yourself get ruffled. Any fool can lose his temper but it takes a wise man to remain equable. Do not answer questions aggressively. Refrain from such openings as 'Aha, I can shoot you down on that one straight away!' Do not give your questioner the impression that his question is stupid. If he is sincere but mistaken he merits courteous attention; if he is trying to be destructive your courteous reply may prevent his query from doing any damage.

VI

Special Occasions

'No one can guarantee success in war, but only deserve it.' (Sir Winston Churchill: *Their Finest Hour*).
'All the business of war, and indeed all the business of life, is to endeavour to find out what you don't know from what you do; that's what I called "guessing what was at the other side of the hill".' (Duke of Wellington).

Case Presentation

We use 'case presentation' to cover any situation where you are trying to persuade any person or group to accept a line of action that you want them to follow. It covers everything from selling Life Assurance to one man up to selling a Pension Scheme to a Board; from persuading your Research Director to send you back to Oxford for a year or not to send you back to Cambridge, up to inducing the Finance Committee to increase your budget by 100 per cent.

If you have to present a case or argument formally but briefly across a table you should go through the same preparation stages as you would if you were to address a large audience in a lecture theatre. You will need to take some extra steps; but all the items mentioned in this book apply just as much to the 'across the table' or 'over the desk' presentation to a small group or to one man as they do to a 'from the rostrum' address to a hall filled with listeners.

82

Two problems in particular must receive most careful thought as you prepare a case : change and competition. If you are advocating a change in current practice, an innovation of some kind, a departure from known and comfortably familiar paths, you must prepare to meet the inertia or the active resistance of the many for whom the *status quo* spells security. You must be ready also to deal with competition. If you are making a claim for resources, some other claimant may oppose you. If you are proposing a line of action that will benefit one part of an operation, or bring fresh power and prestige to one section of an organization, rival areas will suspect your motives and prepare to battle for their own interests. If you have seen the advantages of one course of action, people with different backgrounds and other viewpoints will propose alternatives.

If you are to deal competently with these problems you should prepare the *opposition* case as early as possible. 'As early as possible' for two reasons. Once your views on how to put your case forward have crystallized, you will find it harder to see weaknesses in your ideas; even if you do see them, you may be irrationally reluctant to amend or reverse your approach to take account of the opposition. Conversely, the earlier you prepare the opposition case, the sooner are you likely to see how you should modify the tentative ideas you already have for the case you propose. So write down the drawbacks of your scheme, and not just its advantages. Consider thoroughly what alternative schemes might be suggested by rivals or opponents, and adopt as many as you can of the strong points of these schemes.

The process of considering the opposition case will not only help you to deal with objections when they arise; it will also help you to get your aim clear. You must decide what is vital to your case and what is merely ancillary – what you must fight to keep and what you may throw to the wolves. Thinking about the faults in your own proposal is a useful tool in clarifying your aim, in identifying irrelevancies and highlighting essentials.

As you ponder the problems of overcoming resistance to change, try and put yourself into the position of members of the group who may be adversely affected, or who may fear that they will be adversely affected. Ask yourself : 'If I were old Q, how would I feel if someone made this suggestion? What would worry me about it? Would it be fear of the unknown? Would I be anxious about my own position and prestige? Would I feel resentful at an implication that I had fallen short?'

You will not be able to exclude resistance to change, but you should be able to reduce it if you ask yourself those questions. Just how you bring about the reduction must depend on local knowledge. If you feel that it is 'the unknown' that will cause most trouble, try to find parallel cases where your type of proposal has worked well. If this is impossible, set out clearly the evils that will follow if your scheme is rejected. Given a choice between a risky unknown, and certain bankruptcy, even the most timid and rigid are likely to opt for the unknown. If you feel that resentment may flare as a result of your remarks, try to be tactful. If you have to criticize current practice, do your best to make it clear that you are attacking a problem, not a person; and choose your words with care. Let 'Conjugations for Conferees' (Page 34) be your warning guide.

When you consider the competition you may meet, remember that if you want to really succeed you will have to present your facts so that the people you are trying to persuade *see the benefits* which your scheme provides for them as well as for you. Both you and your auditors should think in terms of the whole system you belong to or are trying to serve. No one element, no sub-system, should try to become more dominant than its contribution to the purposes of the whole requires : the tail should not try to wag the dog. You may be wrongly accused of this if you rely on bare facts, for they may not mean to your audience what they mean to you. Especially where complex or specialist matters have to be put over to laymen, it is not enough to let the facts speak for themselves. They will speak intelligibly to those alone who understand a specialist dialect. You must show clearly the relevance of the facts, and how they relate significantly to the needs and interests of the potential clients. The expert can too easily ignore the need to take his audience by the hand through the facts, figures and relationships which are so clear and obvious to him.

'Obvious' is a danger word : beware of it. If you find yourself thinking or saying 'obviously', stop and ask yourself, 'Obvious to whom and in what conditions?' No thing is obvious in its own right : it can only be obvious, 'open to eye or mind, clearly perceptible, palpable, indubitable', as the Concise Oxford Dictionary puts it – it can only be obvious to those whose eyes have already been opened, to those who have the necessary framework of knowledge or the appropriate set of beliefs. The specialist or enthusiast who is preparing a case must therefore constantly ask himself, 'How can I get across to my listeners just *why* these items matter, what they indicate, how they link up with other factors which are relevant to and understood by this group?' He must remember that 'X is important and interesting' often means 'X is important and interesting *to me*'. But 'to me' is not enough. If 'X' matters, the specialist must go on to make it important and interesting to the people whose opinions he is trying to sway.

One important decision remains for you to take before you come to present your case formally to a meeting: should you contact any of the members in advance? You may want to warn anyone who might oppose the views you intend to put forward; or you may want to enlist support.

It may sound strange to say, 'You may want to warn potential opponents'. Surely they are more likely to be defeated if you hit them without notice? The difficulty is that only in warfare can you hope for a victory that will not be reversed later – and even unconditional surrender may turn out to be conditional! If your potential opponents are not warned, then they will probably react in the negative way that so many of us adopt when suddenly confronted with a new idea : they will reject it. They will resent your attempt to 'put something across them', and resentful people do not think positively. At the best their comments will be impromptu, and impromptu thoughts are commonly shallow ones.

If you do not warn your potential opponents, you may end up with the worst of both worlds. They may succeed in rejecting your proposal, aided by a feeling among neutral members that you have been underhand or discourteous, or both. Your opponents may manage to postpone the decision to a later meeting, on the perfectly valid grounds that they need time to think about it and collect data. In this case too you will have gained nothing by your inept essay in Gamesmanship. If despite a resentful opposition, your scheme does get approval, the defeated elements are very likely to continue their opposition by the methods of underground warfare known to all experienced executives.

So, brief everyone who needs briefing, or else check with your appointed chairman that he has done so. The briefing can *be* brief by the way : there is no need to give a blow-by-blow forecast of all the points you intend to make, nor to fire off all your bullets before the engagement begins. But do not try to 'win' by a sudden knock-out blow at an unsuspecting rival, unless you can be certain of lasting success.

Just in case of misunderstanding, this advice on briefing the opposition and other interested parties is only meant for circumstances where the opposition is internal, where those opposing belong to the same organization as you do or share a common interest. We are not suggesting that if you are in commercial competition with a rival firm you send them a note of your plan of campaign !

So much for reducing resistance. What should you do positively to gain support before the meeting? The answer here must depend on local convention. Some people and organizations deplore lobbying. They match in disapproval the gentleman who, with sublime contempt, remarked :

'Let it be freely confessed . . . that in every age there have existed those of degraded propensities who, while not going to the length of actually extolling what they purvey, have not scrupled by various insidious wiles to create an atmosphere favourable to their own selfish interests.' (Ernest Bramah : *Kai Lung Beneath The Mulberry Tree*.)

Only a lunatic would lobby there ! But if there is *any* danger that lobbying may be resented, that it may boomerang, then avoid it. 'If in doubt, don't.' If you do lobby, remember that you must prepare for your lobbying interview as if you were presenting a case, for that is exactly what you have to do, though to an audience of one.

87

At last comes the occasion for you to present your carefully prepared case. Usually you should start by giving signposts to the points you intend to cover; if you can write these up, so much the better. Start by making it clear what you are going to propose, what your main theme is. Do this even if the Chairman in his introductory remarks has indicated it already. If you are advocating that your Board establish a programme of management development for managers of certain grades, say so plainly: 'I am going to ask you to approve a programme of management development for all managers in grades X to Y inclusive.' Next say what the main points are. You might include for example:

1. Why is the scheme necessary?
2. What would the programme cover – what would be the content?
3. How much would it cost, and how would you finance it?
4. What are the likely consequences if we do not adopt a management development programme?

You should refer to Page 52 for suggestions on just how to announce these headings: but however you do it, they must be clear – and you must do what you say you are going to do. Some of the sections may be complicated: any section which contains three or four sub-sections probably *is* complicated. So when you come to such a section, first announce the main theme, and then list the sub-sections before you plunge into detail about them.

Finally you arrive at your conclusion. Do not waste it. Here is the place to drive home your key point, to stress the element or elements that you earlier decided must be preserved, must not be thrown to the wolves. If you have been interrupted during your presentation, here is your opportunity to redirect people's attention to the essentials of your argument. Here is the point most likely to be remembered : so do prepare carefully.

This plan of presentation makes no claim to be novel. It is no more than a sophisticated version of the old clergyman's recipe for a good sermon : 'I tell them what I'm going to tell them; then I tell them; then I tell them what I've told them.' But it does mean that people can follow you easily. The signposting technique helps the listener to listen intelligently; it also cuts down the risk that he will intervene with distracting questions about element 3 of your case when you are in the middle of element 1.

The exception to this signposting approach is the occasion when for tactical reasons you want to keep your audience guessing. You may want your listeners to work out their own solutions as you go along. Or you may suspect that if your audience knew where you were leading them, they would shut their minds to your ideas and mentally reject your scheme in advance. In such conditions you naturally present your data step by step without first revealing your full plan. You try to lead your listeners by small, closely reasoned stages until, by the time your destination comes in view, it is too late for the audience to refuse to board your train of thought.

As you prepare, and as you speak, you must behave like a good salesman. The good salesman does not try to say everything about his product. Instead, he selects the key points that matter to his potential customer. Although the good salesman has perfectly adequate knowledge of his product, he does not parade all that knowledge : but he does have it available in case it should be needed. The good salesman is accurate : his facts are correct, his figures bear scrutiny, his arithmetic is right. The good salesman is honest : he will not fall over backwards to suggest improbable objections and minor disadvantages to his customer, but he will point out any important snags; he will then go on to explain why he thinks they can be ignored, or how they can be compensated for. Finally, the good salesman does not win arguments. An old and true saying among salesmen runs : 'Win the argument and lose the sale'. When a customer raises an objection, the good salesman does not lose his temper, nor does he try to brush the question aside. Instead he accepts the objection as important and relevant (which it *is* to the customer) and explains how it can be overcome, or even asks the customer what ways he sees of overcoming it. 'That worried me too, but then I found out that . . .', is far more intelligent and courteous an answer than, 'Good heavens, can't you see that?'

It will be clear now that there is much more to case presentation than getting a good idea ! As we stressed earlier in this book, people differ, and people are emotional as well as rational. Not even a combination of Shakespeare, Machiavelli, Freud and Einstein could guarantee success. But if you follow the pattern we have laid down, you will have done your best. If you want to go further, there are a couple of books you can start with. *Games People Play* will probably help you to understand the motives and recognize the style of certain types of questioner you will meet as you present your cases. Eric Webster's *How to Win the Business Battle* will give you further light-hearted but sound advice on the tactics of persuasion. These are necessary studies, for as Webster himself wrote :

'Getting each individual idea accepted involves having hundreds more ideas about how to put it across. Yet inveterate ideas men are often disturbingly slow to learn this simple lesson. They continue, in the teeth of the evidence, to show child-like faith in their fellow-men's logic, intelligence, goodwill and desire for progress. In consequence, they get persecution instead of promotion, petulance instead of praise, frustration instead of fun.'

Social Speaking

Here's to the maiden of bashful fifteen;
Here's to the widow of fifty;
Here's to the flaunting extravagant quean,
And here's to the housewife that's thrifty.
Let the toast pass,
Drink to the lass,
I'll warrant she'll prove an excuse for the glass.
Sheridan: *The School for Scandal*

One of the curses of living in communities is that people are not content to eat, marry, launch ships, christen children, attain their majority, meet returning astronauts, greet visiting dignitaries, and so on. They have to make a speech about it, around it, or even despite it.

Occasionally some information is conveyed on these occasions; but the main purpose is social and ceremonial. Goodwill is preserved, tradition observed, merit recognized, noses rubbed.

Fortunately for the unfortunates who are called upon to make – and hear – these addresses, they need not be lengthy. But if they have to be done, they may as well be done competently. This involves going through the same steps as for an ordinary talk – the steps detailed in the foregoing pages. The difference comes in the additional sources of material. When people are involved you get your information about them from such sources as *Who's Who,* or the man's secretary. When a ceremony is the subject matter, you contact

91

an authority. When you have to propose a vote of thanks to a speaker, you try to find out from him or his secretary in advance the general line he intends to take; and you look carefully around for items to be avoided at all costs.

Remember that the eminent are rarely stuffy or insecure, so you can include a mild joke at their expense. But the pseudo-eminent, like many politicians and lieutenants of industry, are often very unsure of themselves, not least because the internal imbalances which have driven them on through life to their positions of temporary eminence render them uncertain and suspicious while there! So be careful in making jokes about them.

A final point. If you are unlucky enough to be asked to propose a toast, or lay a foundation stone, or do any similar speaking chore, do remember not to shut up until you have in fact said what you need to say. A surprisingly large number of people have to be reminded by chairmen, neighbours or even wives, that they have got so involved in their oratory that they have forgotten to declare the bridge open, or to propose the vote of thanks, or the retiring committee's health or whatever it is.

Impromptu Speaking

'The curse is come upon me!' cried The Lady of Shalott (Tennyson, *The Lady of Shalott*)

It is reported that a visitor to Chartwell once heard Sir Winston Churchill parading up and down and talking to himself; the explanation given was that he was preparing his impromptu speech for that evening.

That is the best way to deal with this aspect of social life. If you have reason to suspect that someone you can't avoid and don't want to offend may call upon you suddenly to 'say a few words', prepare them in advance! This may happen at business meetings, for example, and you may be able to do yourself some good if you have prepared a few words for the occasion. Similarly, if you work in an office, works, laboratory or anywhere that is visited by groups of informed or uninformed people, you should have a story ready about your work, to give them as the basis for intelligent questions. But do be careful not to 'blind them with science'. Make sure you use terms your visitors understand.

Unfortunately, you cannot always prepare. Like other misfortunes, 'impromptus' may burst on you out of a clear sky on any social occasion. Then you simply have to say *something*. How do you find that something? What can you do?

Here are three tips. First of all, remember that in these social situations nobody expects any brilliant gems or any valuable information; they will be quite content with any amiable social noise. So you can be vague and woolly without much loss of prestige.

Secondly, you can often develop a mental note from which to talk by going as far back into history as possible, and then bringing your story up to the present. You ask yourself, for example, 'When did I first hear of this product, company, subject, person, and in what connection, and what changes have happened since then?' You then follow the chronological plan. If a person is involved, you can also usefully ask yourself, 'What is his involvement with the current situation?' as well as, 'How long ago did he come here, and what was it like here then?'

Thirdly, remember to take your time. Use all the tricks you can think of to fill in with, what actors call 'business'. All these give you time in which to ask yourself, and answer, the questions we have just been discussing. Do not leap to your feet when the chairman suddenly launches his thunderbolt at you : get up slowly. If you wear glasses, remove them and polish them as you look amiably round at your listeners. If you don't wear glasses, take off your watch and put it on the table in front of you. Draw out your 'Mr. Chairman, Ladies and Gentlemen' slowly, and then pause for a drink of water. Don't be afraid to repeat yourself, to use vague abstract terms, and to make broad sweeping statements. You have only to fill in two or three minutes at the most, and with care you can fill half of this with material of the 'Mr Chairman, this is a surprise . . . how very kind of you . . .' type.

If you still feel appalled, console yourself with the thought offered by a Chinese philosopher to an Emperor who asked for a sentence he could say on any occasion. The sentence ran, 'This too shall pass away'; your two-minute impromptu is usually forgotten as soon as heard !

Reading a Paper

'People talk of "reading a paper" to a Society – and, God help the audience – do just that. The written language is different from the spoken word.' (Suggestions for Speakers: *Institute of Biology Journal,* May 1965.)

If you have to read a paper do not model yourself on the orator in *Pickwick Papers* who, at the Eatanswill Election, 'delivered a written speech of half an hour's length, and wouldn't be stopped, because he had sent it all to the *Eatanswill Gazette,* and the *Eatanswill Gazette* had already printed it, every word'.

All too often 'reading a paper' turns out to be exactly what the phrase implies : someone reads word for word from a printed text. Worse still the text is very often available to the audience, most of whom can read anyhow. This is abysmally boring and also an utter waste of what could be a valuable opportunity.

The purpose of having someone report his discovery by reading a paper is partly to give a social cachet to him. But mainly it is to enable people to question him about details, problems associated with the work, and possible future developments. The speaker should therefore limit himself to a brief exposition of his subject, prepared and delivered just like any other talk. He should then hold himself available to answer questions and to receive suggestions from the audience.

VII

Make Sure You Improve

'If to do were as easy as to know what were good to do, chapels had been churches, and poor men's cottages princes' palaces.'
Merchant of Venice, I, ii

'A word fitly spoken is like apples of gold in pictures of silver. As an earring of gold, and an ornament of fine gold, so is a wise reprover upon an obedient ear'
Proverbs 25: 12

You can improve your speaking entirely by your own efforts; but if you can get the co-operation of an intelligent critic you will progress much faster.

Best of all, attend a speaking course; for there you will receive criticism from a professional instructor as well as from your fellow students. If such a course is not available, you may be able to find colleagues who also want to improve their speaking : then you can form a study group. Failing this, just one colleague or a friend can help, or you can press members of your family into service.

These co-operative efforts are much more productive than work done alone, for it is much easier to see faults of form, content and style in someone else's talk than in one's own. When you are giving a talk you almost need to forget yourself and think only of getting your subject matter through to your audience. It is hard for any speaker to criticize himself and forget himself at the same time!

This does not mean that, if you have no one to help, you have to give up all hope of improvement. As we have said, the most important part of a talk is the preparation : the time and effort you put into this largely determine the quality of the end product. Even if you can find no one to criticize you as you speak, you can almost certainly find somebody to look at the plan of your talk, and make suggestions. You can get extra help on problems of structure and signposting from *Reports and How to Write Them.*

It is much harder to improve on personal points – speed, voice and so on – without help. In time you can develop the habit of looking back over a talk and recalling some of the things you did. In the earlier stages of self-help a good tape recorder can help you to highlight faults.

Now for the happier situation where you have critics to help you. The critic must know what to look out for, so his first step can be to read this book. Then he must prepare to criticize methodically and constructively.

The points the critic should look for have been detailed in our previous chapters; before undertaking the role of mentor he must acquaint himself thoroughly with them. Here however are a few guide-lines :

Material
Is it relevant to the aim? Is the amount right – neither too much for the time available, nor too sketchy? Is the balance right – the distribution of material between different aspects of the theme? Is the level of material, its complexity, and the language used, suited to the audience? Are key points emphasized? Are examples used where needed? Is the material interesting? Is it accurate, without overstatements or errors?

Structure

Does the talk have a plan, and is the plan made clear to the audience? Are signposts used, and are they accurate? Are the sections of the talk linked together into a coherent whole? Is the order haphazard, or one which helps the audience to follow?

Are the introduction and conclusion clear, well-presented, apt? Do they distract us from the main theme, or emphasize it?

Presentation

Language : Is it natural? Are specialist terms well explained?

Visual aids : clear, well-prepared, relevant, properly timed?

Attention to audience : remembered or forgotten? How far does the speaker observe listeners, gather clues from their behaviour?

Speed : well controlled, varied, enough pauses?

Voice : alive, controlled, audible, interesting?

Behaviour : helpful in emphasizing points, or distracting?

If you have formed a group, then each member should take a different point of criticism in turn.

Critics should bear two warnings in mind : they should not concentrate on trivialities, and they should not be destructive. Any intelligent listener can quickly learn to identify weak points of presentation. These must be corrected. But the critic must not stop here : he must continue with the harder task of uncovering faults of content, of structure, of continuity. Having uncovered faults, the critic must deal with them as positively as possible. He must be frank, but he must be constructive.

It is destructive to say of someone's choice of material, 'It was no good'. It is constructive to say, 'At such and such a point you could have used an example', or 'There are a lot of details about X, but they didn't form a complete picture : we needed some preliminary signposting'. For the personal points too, it is easy to be destructive. 'You didn't use your hands very well' is nowhere near as useful as 'You could have used your hands at such and such a point to help us understand the shape of Z', but the former is much easier to say!

One last thing we must remind you of : relaxation. This is a way of self-improvement which you can practise by yourself. Once you begin to learn how to become physically relaxed, you will find that your speaking improves. As your nervous tensions reduce, so your personality is enabled to express itself and to enliven your thinking, with beneficial results for both your preparation and your presentation.

As you reach the end of this book you may be wondering how good a speaker you can hope to become. The answer is, almost, 'as good as you deserve'. You may never become first-class, just as you may never develop into a champion racing-car driver, or a brilliant linguist, or a Mr Universe. But these limitations do not mean that you cannot learn to drive competently, or master a foreign tongue adequately, or keep yourself fit and trim. So the fact that Demosthenes is unlikely to have to move over to make room for you in his niche in the Hall of Fame should not discourage you from making the effort needed to develop into a better speaker.

You can certainly become a competent workman-like speaker, provided that you are already capable of walking into a restaurant and ordering a meal or going up to a booking office and buying a railway ticket. Only one thing can hinder you in your aspirations to improve into a thoroughly effective speaker – the belief that there is a trouble-free, effortless way of speaking well. Nothing can replace careful preparation, thoughtful presentation, and continuing effort. 'Work,' said Thomas Carlyle, 'is the grand cure of all the maladies and miseries that ever beset mankind'. For 'mankind' read instead 'speakers and their audiences' and you will have a pretty good maxim to follow.

BOOK LIST

REPORT WRITING

Shearring, H. A., and Christian, B. C. *Reports and How to Write Them* (George Allen & Unwin, Ltd. 1965)

SPEAKING AND VOICE PRODUCTION

Henderson, A. M., *Handbook of Good Speaking* (Barker)
Wallace, C., *The Public Speaker's Pocket Book* (Evans Brothers Ltd, 1961)
Westland, P., *Public Speaking* (English University Press, 1946)

LANGUAGE AND THINKING

Hayakawa, S. I., *Language in Thought and Action* (George Allen & Unwin Ltd, 1965)
Keyes, K. S., Jnr, *How to Improve Your Thinking Ability* (McGraw Hill, 1950)
Gordon, W. J. J., *Synectics* (Harper & Row)

PSYCHOLOGY

Berne, E., *Games People Play* (Penguin Books, 1968)
Webster, E., *How to Win the Business Battle* (Penguin Books, 1967)

RELAXATION

Fink, D. H., *Release from Nervous Tension* (George Allen & Unwin Ltd, 1967)
Knowles, W. P., *New Life Through Breathing* (George Allen & Unwin Ltd, 1966)

USING VISUAL AIDS

Powell, L. S., *A Guide to the Use of Visual Aids* (Bacie, 1967)
Powell, L. S., *A Guide to the Overhead Projector* (Bacie, 1967)

(BACIE is an abbreviation of British Association for Commercial and Industrial Education)

GEORGE ALLEN & UNWIN LTD

Head Office

40 Museum Street, London W.C.1
Telephone: 01-405 8577
Sales, Distribution and Accounts Departments
Park Lane, Hemel Hempstead, Herts.
Telephone: 0442 3244

Athens: 7 Stadiou Street, Athens 125
Auckland: P.O. Box 36013, Auckland 9
Barbados: Rockley New Road, St. Lawrence 4
Bombay: 103/5 Fort Street, Bombay 1
Calcutta: 2850 Bepin Behari Ganguli Street, Clacutta 12
Dacca: Alico Building, 18 Motijheel, Dacca 2
Hornsby, N.S.W.: Cnr. Bridge Road and Jersey Street, 2077
Ibadan: P.O. Box 62
Johannesburg: P.O. Box 23134, Joubert Park
Karachi: Karachi Chambers, McLeod Road, Karachi 2
Lahore: 22 Falettis' Hotel, Egerton Road
Madras: 2/18 Mount Road, Madras 2
Manila: P.O. Box 157, Quezon City, D-502
Mexico:Serapio Rendon 125, Mexico 4, D.F.
Nairobi: P.O. Box 30583
New Delhi: 4/21-22B Asaf Ali Road, New Delhi 1
Ontario: 2330 Midland Avenue, Agincourt
Rio de Janerio: Caixa Postal 2537-ZC-00
Singapore: 248C-6 Orchard Road, Singapore 9
Tokyo: C.P.O. Box 1728, Tokyo 100-91
Wellington: P.O. Box 1467, Wellington, New Zealand

Reports and How to Write them

H. A. SHEARRING   B. C. CHRISTIAN

Reports should transfer ideas from writers to readers clearly and painlessly; too often reports do otherwise and produce little but confusion and frustration.

Writers are often, but not always to blame; readers, especially those who commission reports, are often at fault too. Both writers and readers must recognize and overcome the emotional and intellectual barriers that divide them.

This book sets out clearly what the barriers are and how they can be overcome. Readers and writers of reports will be able to apply its teachings at once to their own work. They will be able to close the unhappy gap which divides them, and will see how to avoid the muddle-headedness which might re-open it.

The authors do not believe that you have to be dull and pompous as a proof that what you say is important; their book is therefore not only helpful and authoritative, it is also lively.

The authors have a long experience of teaching communication techniques to scientists and managers in a variety of industries and countries. This provides them with a down-to-earth approach to writing about the presentation of technical and commercial information.

LONDON : GEORGE ALLEN AND UNWIN LTD